A POCKET GUIDE

DISCOVERING WELSH GRAVES

D0544552

A POCKET GUIDE

DISCOVERING WELSH GRAVES

ALUN ROBERTS

CARDIFF
UNIVERSITY OF WALES PRESS
THE WESTERN MAIL
2002

Published by the University of Wales Press and The Western Mail.

British Library Cataloguing in Publication Data
A catalogue record for this book is available from the British Library

ISBN 0-7083-1792-8

All the photographs, including the one on the front cover, were taken by the author.

Front cover: Treorchy cemetery. The statue on the right is the memorial to Thomas Beynon of Oak Tree Shop, Pentre.

Cover design by Chris Neale
Typeset by the University of Wales Press
Printed in Great Britain by MPG Books Ltd, Bodmin

For

Cynthia and Mags

Contents

Introduction

There can be few sadder sights in the whole of Wales than the small cemetery which adjoins the now derelict Independent chapel at Cymer in the Rhondda valley. Still-elegant memorials and head-stones rise proudly, though increasingly forlornly, out of an ever-thickening carpet of undergrowth stitched together with brambles and littered with beer bottles, tin cans and all the other debris of modern civilization. Would anyone know, or care, that a holder of the Albert Medal, the forerunner of the George Cross, happens to lie in this special place? A few yards away lies the wife of Thomas Williams who, in his grief in 1889, paid the sum of one pound to ensure 'the proper maintenance of this cemetery for ever' – it is thus inscribed on her tomb. Can it be that this modest investment is the only thing impeding the total dismantling of this blighted place? What is clear is that no one now accepts any responsibility for its upkeep, nor feels the need to treat this once cherished corner of the Rhondda with the respect it deserves. No doubt, in time, the cemetery will go the way of Woodgrange Park cemetery in the London borough of Newham, cleared of its human remains to make way for 120 two-bedroomed flats, the decision of the council earning the support of the London *Evening Standard*:

> In the third millennium the time may have come to question the assumption that the dead have automatic rights to occupy much-prized space often needed by the living.

It can, of course, be argued equally cogently that, now more than ever, do we need oases of protected open space in the centre of our anonymous urban landscapes as a reminder, to use the words of the late Auberon Waugh, 'that the world is not entirely made up of flats, offices, shops and other workplaces' (*Daily Telegraph*, 26 March 2000). However, in more solemn vein, he adds that 'the most important function of a cemetery – and this applies most particularly to those which still allow visitors – is its most obvious one: to tell us that we, too, are going to die'.

Fortunately, for whatever reason, people's interest in cemeteries and churchyards seems to remain as strong as ever and not simply in relation to the poignant memorials so tenderly maintained across the world by the Commonwealth War Graves Commission and similar organizations. The great burial grounds of Paris, Père Lachaise, Montmartre and Montparnasse, are major tourist attractions, Père

Lachaise alone attracting two million visitors a year. In New Orleans, organized tours are offered of those cemeteries, or 'cities of the dead' as they are called, considered safe enough to visit. In England there exists a National Federation of Cemetery Friends and many of the major cemeteries in London and elsewhere provide guided tours. There is now even a Cemetery of the Year award, won in its inaugural year by Carlisle. The BBC *History* magazine includes in each issue what amounts to its 'grave of the month', and during the summer of 2002 the stories behind some of the gravestones in the churchyards and cemeteries of Wales were revealed in the HTV series *Talking Stones*.

For many the fascination lies in the architecture, the wonderful array of monumental styles that exists in all the great cemeteries, including those serving the major cities, where local men and women of substance lie in close proximity to their humbler brethren. As long ago as 1831, writing about the new cemetery in Glasgow (*Necropolis Glasguensis with Observations on Ancient and Modern Tombs and Sepulture*), John Strang said this:

> We have seen with what pains the most celebrated nations of which history speaks have adorned their places of sepulture and it is from their funereal monuments that we gather much that is known of their civil progress and of their advancement in taste . . . The tomb has, in fact, been the great chronicler of taste throughout the world.

Undercliffe cemetery, for instance, is a spectacular memorial to the families who made nineteenth-century Bradford the worsted capital of the world. The Behrens, Milligans, Holdens, they are all there, with arguably the greatest of them, Alfred Illingworth, resting in an edifice worthy of an Egyptian pharaoh. St Woolos cemetery, Newport, which opened in 1853, and Cathays cemetery, Cardiff, opened six years later, are equally replete with handsome memorials to the great and good of their local communities.

Not all eminent men and women have elaborate memorials. The resting place of the 5th Baron Harlech near Talsarnau in Gwynedd is a modest affair, while DylanThomas's burial place, in Laugharne churchyard, is marked by a simple white wooden cross (which, of course, makes it immediately recognizable amidst a sea of stone). Moreover, the towering and, one has to say, expensive and sometimes dangerous monuments of the past are no longer fashionable, or even encouraged. As a *Times* editorial recently lamented:

now strict ecclesiastical regulations govern the modern memorial's design. Fierce bureaucrats patrol the boundaries of taste. As a result acres of Britain have been regimented into dreary Modernist cities in miniature, into soulless expanses of harsh, shiny granite, sterile wildernesses of stumps.

Fortunately, for a large number of visitors to churchyards and cemeteries, the main objective is not to admire the architecture but to commune with notable men and women of the past and perhaps reflect on the words of Thomas Gray in his 'Elegy Written in a Country Churchyard': 'The paths of glory lead but to the grave.' In Douglas Greenwood's view, 'to reach back over the centuries to an understanding of our heritage and our roots, it is necessary to seek the resting places of the famous, those who have shaped our past'.

Visitors to churchyards and cemeteries also learn much about the circumstances of the countless ordinary men and women, and children, who have lived and died before us. Some years ago Ronald Fletcher wrote a most interesting and poignant book, *In a Country Churchyard* (1978), in which, through a number of life stories hidden in the country churchyards of East Anglia, he reminded his readers that:

a country churchyard is more than just a burial place for the dead. It is a place which reminds us of a living tradition, the people and communities of the past which made us what we are.

St Brynach's churchyard in Nevern, Pembrokeshire, is just such a place. By the porch stands the famous tenth- or eleventh-century Celtic cross, which tells visitors of the close links between west Wales and Ireland in the Middle Ages. Elsewhere in the churchyard are many indications of the fragility of human existence among generations gone by, not least the tombstone which carries the following poignant epitaph:

Anna Letitia and George, infant children of the Rev. D. Griffiths, Vicar 1783–1834.

They tasted of life's bitter cup,
Refused to drink the potion up,
But turned their little heads aside,
Disgusted with the taste, and died.

No visitor to Eglwysilan churchyard, above Abertridwr, can fail to be moved by the graves of miners killed in the Senghennydd mine disaster of 1913 and in other disasters of that time. The sight of the rows of graves in the hillside cemetery above Aberfan, commemorating, in the historian Dai Smith's biting phrase, 'the foulest coalfield disaster of them all', still takes the breath away. At Cefn Golau cemetery, lonely and eerie in the hills above Tredegar, the mournful graves of cholera victims stand, or mainly lean, some distance away from the rest, for fear of contagion. And can there ever have been a more graphic account of a human tragedy than this, recorded on the imposing memorial, in St Woolos cemetery, to the thirty-nine labourers (or 'Soldiers of Industry') killed in the trench disaster at the New Docks Works, Newport on 2 July 1909?

Soldiers of Industry, who fought so well
Against the powers of Earth and Sea and Sky,
Beaten at last – crushed, shattered – where you fell
Deep-buried in a mighty grave you lie.

O valiant soldiers, where your captains led
There you advanced, grimly your foes to meet –
The shore's salt oose, the clay's alluvial bed,
The tide, the sand. But now you taste defeat.

Yours the defensive warfare of the spade,
Yours to set back the limits of the deep,
Yours to delve far. But in the trench you made
You fought your last with nature – and so sleep.

Nomads of Industry reach home at last;
At length the soldier has no foe to foil.
Your wandering and your fighting now are past.
Peace to the fallen in the ranks of toil!

The Christian names of twelve of those commemorated were not known.

At their best, graveyards are peaceful havens where all forms of nature flourish. The Cardiff Leisure and Amenities Department, like those of several other towns and cities in Britain, has produced a splendid brochure, *The Cathays Cemetery Heritage Trail*, celebrating the attractions of a cemetery which, even at the time of its opening in 1859, was predicted to become the 'principal walk of the citizens of Cardiff'. The brochure not only identifies the many interesting graves to be found in the cemetery, commemorating the shipping magnates of the great days of the Cardiff docks as well as humbler folk, such as the young domestic servant who met her death in a freak ballooning accident. It also describes the trees, plants, animals and birds which share occupancy with the people of Cardiff. As the brochure says, 'the vast number of interesting memorials and the changing character of the cemetery through the seasons make Cathays a place worth visiting time and time again'.

However, as has already been suggested, for most people the main purpose of visiting churchyards and cemeteries is, in the words of Michael Kerrigan, to 'gawp at the graves of (more or less) famous people', and there appears to be a market for books directing visitors to where they may be found. Four books worth mentioning are Douglas Greenwood's *Who's Buried Where in England* (1982; new edition 1999), Brian Bailey's *Churchyards of England and Wales* (1987), Michael Kerrigan's *Who Lies Where: A Guide to Famous Graves* (1995), and *Discovering Famous Graves* (1998) by Lyn Pearson. While exempting Greenwood from criticism as his book focuses specifically on England (apart from the French burial places of some of our medieval monarchs), the coverage of Wales by the others is disappointing. Bailey, who concentrates on churchyards, cites only eight graves in Wales as worthy of mention, while Pearson, in a broader review of graveyards, embracing both churchyards and cemeteries, refers to fifteen names altogether, four of whom have no resting place at all – a poor crop indeed. Wales does slightly better in Kerrigan's book, with a still measly twenty-six entries. My guide refers to over 350 Welsh graves of the famous, and not-so-famous, and the number could easily have been greater, but one has to draw a line somewhere.

The more or less essential prerequisite for inclusion in this guide is that the subjects were buried in Wales. Most of those included were Welsh, but by no means all. Thomas Bowdler was not Welsh nor was Herbert Gladstone. On the other hand, many very eminent Welsh men and women do not, strictly speaking, qualify for inclusion in this particular book because they were buried outside Wales – people like Sir Thomas Picton, the only Welshman to be buried in St Paul's Cathedral, Richard Burton, buried in Switzerland and, of course, Hedd Wyn, laid to rest near Ypres – though occasionally an opportunity is taken to refer to them. Others have been cremated, their ashes scattered to the winds, but the book does refer to some of them. No one knows when, or where Wales's greatest national hero, Owain Glyndŵr, died, or was buried. One Welsh chronicler wrote:

'The majority say that he died, the soothsayers say he did not.' Nowadays, people tend to accept the theory that he died in or around 1415, having lived with his daughter and her family in Herefordshire where he was buried. The claims of those who argue that the Virgin Mary is buried at Llanerchymedd in Anglesey have not been accepted.

Assuming that the essential qualification for entry was met, how were those included in this book actually chosen? Nothing is more certain than that there are omissions, some inexcusable, others inadvertent and many simply a reflection of one person's perspective or prejudice. One hopes that the most obvious candidates have found their way on to the following pages. The characters that turn up in all the other books are, of course, here – Robert Owen of Newtown, Dylan Thomas, Richard Wilson, Elihu Yale, David Lloyd George – as are those who really should be in all the other books but are not – notables such as Bishop William Morgan, Griffith Jones, Dic Penderyn and Sir Owen Morgan Edwards, to name only four. The general criterion for inclusion is that there is something interesting to record about a grave's occupant, whether he or she was celebrated or unknown, bearing in mind that some people, nowadays quite unremembered, were once household names. Who today has heard of Arthur Linton, whose funeral, in 1896, was one of the largest ever seen in Aberdare? Thomas Heslop was, by any yardstick, a nonentity but he earns a place in this guide by being the last person in Wales who was killed in a duel. Since this is a book about Wales it is hardly surprising that many of those included were politicians, preachers, hymn-writers and poets but an attempt has been made to include categories of people often under-represented in compilations of this sort, particularly sportsmen and, indeed, women.

The book is the product of a lot of reading, too much to sum-marize in a full bibliography, though some key works must be mentioned. The essential starting point for a study of this sort must be the authoritative *Dictionary of Welsh Biography down to 1940* and its successor volume which takes the date forward to 1970, both produced in Welsh and English. Among the great merits of these works is the fact that many of the entries refer to the burial place of the person described. The superb *New Companion to the Literature of Wales* (1998), compiled by Meic Stephens, which also has a Welsh-language edition (*Cydymaith i Lenyddiaeth Cymru*, new edition 1997), includes many of the same people and provides valuable suggestions for further reading. Meic Stephens is also the author of the extremely useful *The Literary Pilgrim in Wales* (2000), which gives the resting places of some of the people included in his guide. The best one-volume *History of Wales* is that produced in Welsh (*Hanes Cymru*, 1990) and English (1993) by John Davies for Penguin. Four excellent volumes in the History of Wales series produced by the Clarendon Press and the University of Wales Press have so far appeared: R. R. Davies, *Conquest, Coexistence and Change, Wales 1063–1415* (1987), Glanmor Williams, *Recovery, Reorientation and Reformation, Wales c.1415–1642* (1987), Geraint H. Jenkins, *The Foundations of Modern Wales 1642–1780* (1987), and K. O. Morgan, *Rebirth of a Nation, Wales 1880–1980* (1981). The monographs in the Writers of Wales series, published by the University of Wales Press, are well worth reading, as are the splendidly illustrated volumes in the Bro a Bywyd series, written in Welsh about some of the nation's cultural giants of the last century. Jan Morris's book *The Matter of Wales: Epic Views of a Small Country* (1984) is a constant delight. Mention must also be made of the truly excellent series of programmes on HTV, *Wild Tracks*, presented by Trevor Fishlock, which put me on to a number of graves which I might otherwise not have encountered.

The library at the University of Wales conference centre, Gregynog, has been a veritable treasure trove. So have several excellent public libraries throughout Wales, and the microfilm newspaper collection in the local studies department of the Cardiff Central Library has been an invaluable source of information about the funerals and subsequent burials, or otherwise, of many of those referred to in this book. I am grateful to staff in several county archive/local history departments for answering, by e-mail and in other ways, all manner of queries. One thing that makes this book a little different from most others of its type is the inclusion of fairly precise guidance as to where the people are actually buried, and in order to achieve this I have visited (and photographed) most of the graves mentioned. Warm thanks are offered to all the superintendents of cemeteries and crematoria and their staff, vicars and curates, Nonconformist ministers and members of the public who have so helpfully answered my letters and even conducted me to the actual locations. For instance, I remember when, one rainy afternoon, a lady locked up her post office in Llanfair, Gwynedd, and took me into the churchyard across the road to show me the grave of Siân Owen, the central character in that celebrated painting, *Salem*. I am also grateful to the Dean of St Davids Cathedral and to the appropriate authorities of the Church in Wales for the churches of

St Michael's (Myddfai), St Padarn (Llanbadarn Fawr), Ruabon, and St Tegai (Llandygái) for permission to include the photographs on pp. 90, 27, 32, 129 and 58

It is a pleasure to thank Susan Jenkins, Liz Powell and particularly Ruth Dennis-Jones at the University of Wales Press for their expert advice and enthusiastic support in the preparation of this volume. I am dedicating the book to two people; to my wife, Cynthia, whose constant encouragement and patient smile, even when I have returned home soaking wet after roaming around churchyards in the pouring rain, have meant a great deal; and to my sister Margaret who, probably rightly, attributes my apparent obsession with graveyards to the influence of our late father, who could never pass one without taking a look inside. But then, he was a Methodist minister after all.

A word about the organization of entries in this book. Bearing in mind the frequency with which local government boundaries in Wales seem to change, it has been tempting to list all those appearing in this book in alphabetical order of town or village. However, if the book is to serve as a practical guide for grave-hunters there is undoubted benefit in grouping people within convenient geographical areas, and the current local government boundaries (subdivided in the cases of Gwynedd and Powys) are as useful as any other. Finally, where a grave is referred to as being to the right or left of a place of worship it is assumed that the visitor is facing the front of the building.

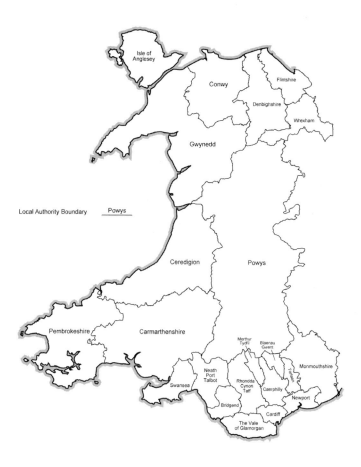

Isle of
Anglesey

Conwy

Flintshire

Denbighshire

Wrexham

Gwynedd

Local Authority Boundary   Powys

Ceredigion

Powys

Pembrokeshire

Carmarthenshire

Merthyr
Tydfil

Blaenau
Gwent

Monmouthshire

Neath
Port
Talbot

Rhondda
Cynon
Taff

Caerphilly

Torfaen

Newport

Swansea

Bridgend

Cardiff

The Vale
of Glamorgan

ANGLESEY

BEAUMARIS

The carved stone covering the grave of **Siwan** (1195–1237), illegitimate daughter of King John and wife of Llywelyn ap Iorwerth, is preserved in the south porch of the parish church. She had originally been laid to rest at Llan-faes but when the friary was dissolved in 1538 the gravestone was moved to Beaumaris. The stone coffin, which came to be used as a horse trough, was reunited with the cover in the nineteenth century.

BRYNSIENCYN

Sir Ellis Jones Ellis-Griffith (1860–1926), one of the most prominent members of the Welsh Liberal Party, is buried in Llanidan churchyard. A Cambridge-educated barrister who was altogether too posh and uxorious for Lloyd George (he called him 'an old baby'), he was MP for Anglesey from 1895 to 1918 and for Carmarthen 1923–4. He became chairman of the Welsh Parliamentary Liberal Party in 1911 for a year, before joining the government as Under-Secretary at the Home Office, taking a prominent part in steering the Welsh Church Disestablishment Bill through the House of Commons. He bitterly attributed his unexpected defeat in the 'Khaki' election to 'Church, Conscription, Congregationalists, Calumny'.

HOLYHEAD

Maeshyfryd cemetery (section 5, grave number 745) is the resting place of **Cledwyn Hughes** (1916–2001), **Lord Cledwyn of Penrhos**, Labour MP for Anglesey from 1951 to 1979, Secretary of State for Wales from 1966 to 1968, Minister of Agriculture from 1968 to 1970 and chairman of the Parliamentary Labour Party from 1974 to 1979. It is said that on one occasion Prime Minister Callaghan made him the leader of a parliamentary delegation to the Soviet Union, arguing that as Cledwyn Hughes spoke Welsh in private the KGB bugs would be useless. During the 1980s he was Labour leader in the House of Lords. He was universally respected across the political spectrum and, in the words of the *Western Mail* following his death, 'he was, and remains, a fine example of how politics need not be a nasty, brutish business'. Also in the cemetery is a memorial to ninety-nine members of the crew of the submarine *Thetis*, which sank off the Great Orme in June 1939 while undergoing trials; only four crewmen escaped. Forty-four are actually buried here. The salvaged vessel was later recommissioned and, renamed the *Thunderbolt*, served during the Second World War before being sunk by enemy action.

LLANDDONA

In the north of the churchyard lies **Robert Everett** (1902?–42), jockey and fighter pilot, who rode the 1929 Grand National winner, Gregalach, at odds of 100–1. He was killed in January 1942 when his Hurricane crashed on a nearby beach.

LLAN-FAES

Just on the left of the entrance to St Catherine's churchyard is a substantial memorial marking the resting place of **John Elias** (1774–1841), the finest and most influential preacher of his day. Through the gifts of oratory and graphical imagery he could reduce his open-mouthed congregations to a state of fear and trembling in their thousands. On one occasion, Elias even reduced the formidable Marquess of Anglesey, a hero of the battle of Waterloo, to tears which 'ran down his face in drops as large as peas'. He was a political hardliner, opposing all the main liberal movements of his day. He regarded Catholic emancipation with dread. Harking back to the reign of 'Bloody Mary', he once said: 'I believe that our children, if not indeed we ourselves, will live to see the stake being raised in the streets of Llangefni so that the Christians of this island may be burnt for their faith.' For his dogmatic attitude he was, ironically, known to many as the 'Anglesey Pope'. A few feet away is the grave of the controversial Calvinistic Methodist minister **John Williams**, Brynsiencyn (1854–1921), another popular orator. Unlike many Nonconformist preachers he keenly supported British participation in the First World War and for a while was Lloyd George's greatest recruiting officer. By the end of the war over 10 per cent of the Welsh population (over 250,000) had served in the armed forces, 10 per cent of whom were killed in action. As the casualties mounted, so Williams's standing collapsed.

LLANFECHELL

In the cemetery of Ebenezer chapel, under a Celtic cross, lies **Brigadier-General Sir Owen Thomas** (1858–1923). After establishing a reputation as an agricultural expert he became a highly regarded soldier, and was responsible for training the north Wales recruits into the army during the First World War, for which he received a knighthood in 1917. Such was his personal popularity within his native county that, as a highly unlikely Labour candidate, he managed to defeat the formidable Liberal MP, Sir Ellis Jones Ellis-Griffith, in the 1918 general election, and to beat another Liberal in 1922, this time standing as an Independent. Shortly afterwards he died and his funeral was one of the largest ever seen in Anglesey, the procession of 200 cars and 3,000 mourners stretching for two miles.

LLANFAIR PWLLGWYNGYLL

An imposing Celtic cross at the far north-west of the church-yard marks the grave of **Sir John Morris-Jones** (1864–1929), the great Welsh scholar who was professor of Welsh at the University College of North Wales, Bangor, and who, in 1913, wrote the standard work on the Welsh language, *A Welsh Grammar, Historical and Comparative*. On the south side, in an elevated position, is a memorial to seventeen men who died from injuries sustained during the construction of the nearby Britannia Bridge between 1846 and 1850, and to one who died of typhoid fever. The names of two more who died during the reconstruction of the bridge in 1972 and 1973 have been added since.

The 1st Marquess of Anglesey (1768–1854), second in command to Wellington at the battle of Waterloo, where he lost a leg, lived at Plas Newydd nearby and is commemorated by a magnificent column, completed (apart from the statue) in 1817. However, following his death in London he was buried in Lichfield Cathedral.

LLANGADWALADR

In the nave of the church is the oldest royal gravestone in Britain, that of **Cadfan** (died about AD 625), ruler of Gwynedd and described in the Latin inscription as *sapientisimus opinateimus omnium regum* (the wisest and most renowned of all kings).

MENAI BRIDGE

The beautifully situated graveyard on Church Island in the parish of Llandysilio is the resting place of **Sir Cynan Evans-Jones** (1895–1970), **Cynan**, the only person to be elected Archdruid of Wales twice, and more than anyone else responsible for the colourful spectacle that characterizes the modern National Eisteddfod of Wales. He once described the Gorsedd of Bards as the 'National Pageant of Wales'. He is buried about twenty-five yards beyond the second turning to the left along the path leading right from the churchyard gate. Not far away lies another major figure in the

John Evans, Y Bardd Cocos, Menai Bridge

cultural life of Wales, **Sir John Edward Lloyd** (1861–1947), author of the pioneering *A History of Wales to the Edwardian Conquest* in 1911, and first editor of the indispensable *Dictionary of Welsh Biography down to 1940.* Moving from the sublime to the ridiculous, also buried in the churchyard, down the slope at the east end of the ancient church of St Tysilio, is the seriously eccentric **John Evans** (1823?–88), better known as **Y Bardd Cocos** (the cockle bard). In poetry terms he was the nearest Welsh equivalent to the Scottish writer of doggerel, the celebrated William McGonagall. His best-known verse commemorated the stone lions erected at each end of the Britannia Bridge linking Anglesey to the mainland:

Pedwar llew tew	(Four fat lions
Heb ddim blew	Without any hair
Dau 'rochor yma	Two on this side
A dau 'rochor drew.	And two over there.)

PENMYNYDD
In the church of St Gredifael is an alabaster table-tomb marking the final resting place of **Gronw Fychan** (died 1382), great-great-uncle of Henry VII and friend of the Black Prince.

RHOSCOLYN
In the churchyard of the beloved village where he had a retirement home lies **Sir Patrick Abercrombie** (1879–1957), the leading British town planner of his day. He was one of the founders of the Council for the Preservation of Rural England, and was best known for his Greater London Plan (1944) which advocated the use of green belts and satellite towns to limit the growth of post-war London.

BLAENAU GWENT

EBBW VALE
In the town cemetery (section K, row 4, grave 14) lies **John Henry Williams** (1886–1953), the most decorated Welsh non-commissioned officer of all time. Serving with the South Wales Borderers during the First World War he received the Distinguished Conduct Medal for action at Mametz Wood in 1916, the Military Medal and Bar for action at Pilkem Ridge and Armentières respectively, both in 1917, and the Victoria Cross (VC) 'for the most conspicuous bravery and

devotion to duty on the night of the 7th/8th October 1918, during the attack on Villers Outreaux'. He received all four decorations from King George V at Buckingham Palace on 22 February 1919, the first occasion on which the king had decorated the same person four times in one day. During the ceremony, one of his wounds opened up and he required immediate treatment before he could leave the palace. In the same year he was awarded the Medaille Militaire by the French government. After the war he worked as a rent collector for the town council, and as a commissionaire in the local steelworks. A photograph was once taken of him standing with the other Welsh John Williams who had won his VC at the battle of Rorke's Drift. Some way beyond Williams (in section L, row 11, grave number 14), lies **Sir Eugene Cross** (1896–1981), a local boy who rose from nothing to become the works manager at the local iron and steel works. He was a magistrate for over thirty years, a member of the Welsh Regional Hospital Board and a noted supporter of good causes. The town park, the home of Ebbw Vale rugby club, is named after him. Down the slope from Sir Eugene there is a group of old gravestones including one, by a bush, marking the resting place of one **Esther John** who died in 1866, aged twenty-four, and the chilling word 'cholera' can still be clearly deciphered.

On the road out of Ebbw Vale towards Beaufort, in a small park next to the Beaufort Arms, is a memorial (it may also be his grave) to **John Emlyn Jones** (1818–73), **Ioan Emlyn**, a respected literary figure in his day and the minister of the town's Nebo Baptist chapel (now demolished) from 1853 to 1861. His most famous poem is 'Bedd y Dyn Tlawd' (the poor man's grave) which, according to a writer of the time, 'will remain memorable among the poems of Wales for its pathos, simplicity and heart-touching effect'.

Neither **Aneurin Bevan** (1897–1960), the local MP ('I never used to regard myself so much as a politician as a projectile discharged from the Welsh valleys') and creator of the National Health Service, nor his wife **Jennie Lee** (1904–88), Baroness Lee of Asheridge, have a resting place, their ashes being scattered on the hills above Tredegar. However, just off the A4047 between Ebbw Vale and Tredegar is a memorial to Aneurin, in the form of a stone circle. The largest of the four stones represents Aneurin Bevan and bears the inscription:

It was here
Aneurin Bevan
spoke to the people
of his constituency and the world.

The other three stones represent the three boroughs making up his constituency.

TREDEGAR

Cholera graveyard, Tredegar

The great Welsh poet Idris Davies loved visiting graveyards and one of his most evocative poems is about Cefn Golau cemetery, up on the moors between Rhymney and Tredegar. It is an eerie and windswept place where Aneurin Bevan's father, David, and nineteenth-century victims of cholera lie buried, though some distance apart, the cholera graveyard being located on bleak moorland well away from the perimeter wall, for fear of contagion. Indeed, when cholera first struck the area in 1832, a circular was issued instructing local places of worship that their graveyards were 'closed against those who died from the cholera'. This is the epitaph to **Thomas James** who died during the second major outbreak, in 1849, aged twenty:

> One night and day I bore great pain
> To try for cure was all in vain
> But God knew what to me was best
> Did ease my pain and give me rest.

7

The headstone of **William Thomas**, wheelwright at the Tredegar Ironworks, who died, aged thirty-eight, on 21 October 1832 – 'the first who died of the cholera and was interred in this burial ground' (Cefn Golau) – is now preserved in the Tredegar Local History Society Museum, adjoining the public library.

BRIDGEND

BRIDGEND
Walter Coffin (1784–1867), the pioneer of the coal industry in the Rhondda valley, who was said to own everything in Dinas 'except the souls of men' is buried in the Unitarian chapel graveyard, Park Street. Unfortunately, since most of the tombstones were removed and the area tarmacked in 1972 his exact whereabouts are no longer marked. Rather hysterically, Lady Bute considered his election as Liberal MP for Cardiff from 1852 to 1857 as representing 'the ascendancy of revolutionary principles'. In fact, Wales's first Non-conformist MP never once addressed the House of Commons during the whole time he was there.

COYCHURCH
In the south-eastern section of St Crallo's churchyard lies **Thomas Richards** (1710–90), curate of the parish of Coychurch for over forty years and described by Iolo Morganwg as 'poor, modest and bashful, though learned'. A largely self-taught scholar, in 1753 he published what was undoubtedly the best Welsh to English dictionary of the period, the *Antiquae Linguae Britannicae Thesaurus*. A plaque was unveiled by Lord Tonypandy inside the church in 1990 to commemorate the bicentenary of Thomas Richards's death.

LLANGYNWYD
Inside St Cynwyd's church, near to the altar, lies **Ann Maddocks** (1704–27), the 'Maid of Cefn Ydfa', the central figure in one of Wales's most poignant love stories about a girl who was married off to a local solicitor rather than marrying her true love **Wil Hopcyn** (1700–41), a plasterer not thought to be good enough for her. After Ann's death, possibly from a broken heart, the distraught Wil, something of a local poet, is said to have written the plaintive love song 'Bugeilio'r Gwenith Gwyn' (watching the ripening wheat) in

commemoration of these sad events. He died, unmarried and a pauper, fourteen years later, and is buried near the western yew tree in the churchyard. Between here and the church stands an elegant obelisk marking the grave of **Vernon Hartshorn** (1872–1931), Labour MP for Ogmore, 1918–31, and the first Welsh miner to achieve Cabinet rank, serving as Postmaster General in the first Labour government in 1924. He became Lord Privy Seal in the second Labour administration with the hopeless task of tackling unemployment, but died before making any impact on this problem. Buried a few feet away is another local celebrity, **Brinley Richards** (1904–81), winner of the National Eisteddfod Chair in 1951 and Archdruid from 1972 to 1975, the first lawyer to be appointed to the position. Near the church door is a splendid brown marble spire over the grave of perhaps the most celebrated vicar of Llangynwyd, **Samuel Jones** (1628–97). A committed Puritan, he was appointed not by the bishop but on the authority of the Lord Protector in 1657 and, following the Restoration, he was deprived of his living for refusing to subscribe to the Act of Uniformity. He continued to live in the area for the rest of his life, establishing at his home at Brynllywarch the first dissenting academy in Wales, where Nonconformist ministers such as Rees Price, father of the great political philosopher Dr Richard Price, were trained.

PORTHCAWL

Not far from the entrance to Newton churchyard on its southern side is the striking Bracchi family plot, containing the remains of **Giacomo Bracchi** (1860?–1940). Originally from Bardi in northern Italy, he pioneered the 'Bracchi' shops, the ice-cream shops and cafés which became such a familiar feature in the high streets of the valley towns of south Wales from the 1890s onwards. By the south wall of the churchyard lies **William Evans Hoyle** (1855–1926), the first director of the National Museum of Wales, from 1909 to 1924.

Bracchi family, Porthcawl

In Porthcawl public cemetery lies **Sir Leslie Joseph** (1908–92), the millionaire businessman who put Porthcawl on the map through the development of Coney Beach and Trecco Bay. At the time of the Festival of Britain he became managing director of Battersea Park Pleasure Gardens, turning a failing business into a profitable venture, earning a knighthood in the process. His grave may be found by proceeding down the central path of the cemetery. It is located to the left of the path immediately beyond the section reserved for ashes. On the far right-hand side of the cemetery, in line with the ashes section, is the grave of the author's grandfather, **David Evans** (1880–1965), the writer of the great Welsh hymn 'O ganu bendigedig' (O blessed song of glory). A native of Blaenpennal in deepest Cardiganshire he wrote the words at the age of nineteen and submitted the piece to *Trysorfa y Plant* where it appeared under the pseudonym Aeronian. Wittingly or unwittingly, the editor of the magazine, Thomas Levi, received the credit for it for many years, perhaps because the person who set the words to music (to the tune 'Côr Caersalem') was none other than Levi's good friend Joseph Parry. 'Defend our children from evil doctors and medical drug abuse' is the poignant inscription on a nearby grave of a twelve-year-old girl who died in 1975, 'a victim of the medical profession'.

CAERPHILLY

CWMFELINFACH
In the small cemetery adjoining Babell chapel, under an elegant column, lies **William Thomas** (1832–78), **Islwyn**, considered among the greatest of nineteenth-century Welsh poets. His reputation mainly rests on two epic poems written in the 1850s, each entitled 'Y Storm' (the storm) and each about 6,000 lines in length. Much of his work was influenced by the sudden death of his fiancée, Anne Bowen, in 1853, and although he married Martha Davies in 1864 he never got over the loss of his first true love. It is reported that on his deathbed Islwyn thanked Martha for all she had done for him: 'You have been very kind. I am going to Anne now.'

GROES-WEN
Near the top of the cemetery adjoining the historic Groes-wen chapel stands a substantial obelisk marking the grave of **Evan Jones** (1820–52). Better known as **Ieuan Gwynedd**, a sickly

Congregationalist minister, he became a national hero in Wales because of his passionate criticism of the 'Llyfrau Gleision', the Blue Books containing the report of the educational commissioners appointed to examine the state of education in Wales (1847). Under the patronage of Lady Llanover he also became editor of the first, albeit short-lived, Welsh publication designed for the women of Wales, *Y Gymraes* (The Welshwoman). Its objective was to create 'faithful girls, virtuous women, thrifty wives and intelligent mothers'. Unfortunately, Ieuan Gwynedd did not live to see the success of his crusade, dying at the early age of thirty-two.

Groes-wen cemetery came to be known as the 'Westminster Abbey of Wales' because of the large number of prominent Nonconformist ministers resting there, including, a few feet from Ieuan Gwynedd, the great **William Williams**, **Caledfryn** (1801–69), buried under a striking memorial bearing his face in bas-relief. Poet, critic, a major influence in the development of the National Eisteddfod and an opponent of the total abstinence campaign as an infringement of individual liberty, he was described at the time of his death as 'a household word among the Welsh nation'.

Caledfryn, Groes-wen

Inside the chapel itself, behind the pulpit, is a memorial tablet designed by Sir William Goscombe John to **William Edwards** (1719–89), pastor of the chapel from 1749 to 1789. He is best remembered as the architect of the bridge crossing the river Taff at Pontypridd, built in 1756 and, at the time, the bridge with the longest single span in Europe. He is buried in Eglwysilan churchyard, a mile or so west of Groes-wen, his grave marked by a chest tomb a few feet from the porch of the church. Several of the 439 miners killed in the Senghennydd mine disaster of 1913 are also buried in the churchyard.

RHYMNEY

About a hundred yards (to the right) along the main path on the right, leading from the entrance to Rhymney cemetery, stands a headstone carrying the epitaph 'Ni caiff [*sic*] yn anghof byth' (he will

11

never be forgotten). Within the grave lie the ashes of one of the greatest Welsh poets of the twentieth century, **Idris Davies** (1905–53), author of the celebrated poetry collections *The Angry Summer*, *Tonypandy and other poems* and *Gwalia Deserta*, in which appear those defiant words by Dai and Shinkin, standing in Charing Cross Road: 'We shall remember 1926 until our blood is dry.'

CARDIFF

CATHAYS

When Cathays cemetery was opened in 1859 the *Cardiff Times*

John Cory, Cathays

believed that 'it would form the principal walk of the inhabitants of Cardiff'. It certainly became the most fashionable resting place for many of its leading citizens. **John Cory** (1823–91) was the head of one of two Cardiff commercial dynasties with the same name and both originating in the west of England. This one hailed from Padstow in Cornwall, but as the local river began to silt up he moved his shipping business to Cardiff where it flourished mightily. By the end of the century, a few years after his death, the family firm, John Cory and Sons and Company, had become one of the leading tramp-ship owners in the country. He is buried under an elegant memorial in section M of the cemetery. His second son, **Sir Herbert Cory** (1857–1933), MP for Cardiff from 1915 to 1924 and the director of more than thirty-five companies, played a great part in

the development of the village of Tongwynlais on the northern edge of Cardiff, and the district of Coryton (junction 32 of the M4) is named after him. Considering his local eminence, his grave (plot

W 920), marked by a plain concrete headstone, is so unobtrusive it can easily be missed.

The same cannot be said of the handsome memorial in section P to **Sir William James Thomas** (1867–1945), a major coalowner and director of the Great Western Railway Company, a lavish benefactor, particularly of health-related causes and medical education in Wales, who received the Freedom of the City of Cardiff in 1915. The elaborate memorial to **William James Tatem** (1868–1942) is located in section L (plot 1699) of the cemetery. From humble beginnings in Devon he built up one of the largest fleets of steam ships operating out of Cardiff, contributing greatly to the city's prosperity as the world's largest coal exporter before the First World War. He was also a passionate supporter of 'the Turf'; during the inter-war years he became one of the country's leading racehorse owners, his stable winning all five Classic races, including the Derby, in 1919, the year when Tatem (by now elevated to the peerage as Baron Glanely of St Fagans) headed the list of winning owners. Tatem received his title at a time when the sale of honours was endemic. There is a story, which may or may not be true, that he gave the treasurer of Lloyd George's political fund a cheque for £50,000 signed 'Glanely'; provided he got his title the treasurer would be able to cash the cheque. His favourite expression was, 'If you've got it, flaunt it.' Lord Glanely and another Cardiff shipowner, **Sir William Reardon Smith** (1856–1935) (buried in plot P 971) received the Freedom of the City of Cardiff at the same ceremony in 1928. **John Batchelor** (1820–83), a shipbuilder, was by no means as popular and after his death a local solicitor wrote a highly defamatory piece in the *Western Mail* which landed him in the High Court on a charge of criminal libel. He was acquitted, thereby establishing in law the principle that to libel the dead does not itself constitute an offence. Poor John Batchelor, 'The Friend of Freedom', whose statue in the middle of Cardiff is regularly embellished with beer glasses, traffic cones and the like, is buried in section O (plot 967), near the main entrance, but the grave is now almost totally obscured by a holly tree growing out of it. Moreover, his hearse crashed into a lamp-post in Penarth on the way to his funeral. **Solomon Andrews** (1835–1908) was another self-made man who did not fit easily into the establishment in late-Victorian Cardiff – not that it ever bothered him. He became the leading manufacturer of horse-drawn omnibuses in the country and had extensive business interests in Cardiff, including shops, funeral parlours, coffee taverns and the purveying of patent medicines such as 'Andrews' Grandmother's Embrocation – an old country remedy'. He was a

13

major property developer – the Market Buildings in St Mary's Street still bear his name. He was also largely responsible for making Pwllheli into a holiday resort through the development of the West End estate. It is hardly surprising that his funeral was one of the largest ever seen in Cardiff, since, according to Andrews' biographer, his great-grandson J. F. Andrews, any of his employees who turned out were offered the tempting inducement of either a new suit or an overcoat. He is buried more or less in the middle of Cathays cemetery in section Q (plot 1061).

Two of Britain's finest sportsmen are buried in the cemetery. **James Driscoll** (1880–1925), Peerless Jim, was British and European featherweight boxing champion before the First World War, and was robbed of the World featherweight crown in 1909 on a technicality. Offered an immediate rematch, Driscoll is said to have declined because he had already promised to return to Cardiff to take part in an exhibition fight for charity and he did not want to let the nuns of Nazareth House down. It is hardly surprising therefore that the handsome Celtic cross marking Driscoll's grave in the Roman Catholic section D of the cemetery is inscribed 'erected by Nazareth House in grateful remembrance'. Driscoll's funeral, when 100,000 people lined the streets, is still regarded as the finest ever seen in Cardiff. **Jack Petersen** (1911–90), dubbed the Welsh Carpentier, became British heavyweight champion in 1932 at the age of twenty, the youngest man to win the title, and later gained the Empire crown too. After his early retirement, which probably saved his good looks and gentlemanly bearing, he had a distinguished career in boxing administration, becoming president of the British Boxing Board of Control in 1986. His headstone (section O, plot 1108) actually uses the family surname, Peterson. The fine Glamorgan and England batsman **Maurice Turnbull** (1906–44) is not buried in the cemetery, though his name is recorded on the memorial at the family plot (C 1853) of the Turnbulls, prominent Cardiff shipowners, near to the Allensbank Road entrance on the left-hand side. Major Turnbull was killed in action in Normandy and lies in the Bayeux War Cemetery. Just beyond the Turnbull plot is a fine memorial incorporating a handsome Celtic cross, provided by a local firm of monumental masons and unveiled on St Patrick's Day, 1999, 'In memory of the victims of the Great Famine in Ireland 1845–1849, and of all Irish people and their descendants who have died in Wales'. Surely one of the most poignant of all the memorials in the cemetery is that commemorating **Louisa Maud Evans**, a domestic servant with

Hancock's circus, whose sad death, on 21 July 1896, at the age of fourteen and a half, is explained on her white headstone in section G:

> On that day she ascended in a balloon from Cardiff, and descended by a parachute into the Bristol Channel. Her body was found washed ashore near Nash (Mon) on the 24th July and was buried here on the 29th.
>
> To commemorate the sad ending of a brave young life this memorial is erected by public subscription.

Buried in the northward extension to Cathays cemetery further along Allensbank Road (section E–F) is one of Wales's greatest ever writers in the Welsh language, **Thomas Rowland Hughes** (1903–49), the author of one of the great modern Welsh hymns, 'Tydi a roddaist liw i'r wawr, a hud i'r machlud mwyn' (Thou gavest colour to the dawning and enchantment to the gentle setting sun). However, his continuing reputation is largely attributable to five novels written in the 1940s, mainly based on the north Wales communities from which he came, probably the best known being *O Law i Law* (From Hand to Hand). In *William Jones* the hero's exasperated outburst to his wife 'Cadw dy blydi *chips*!' (Keep your bloody chips!) caused not a little anguish in good Nonconformist homes. Hughes died prematurely of multiple sclerosis and his headstone carries words of tribute written by the poet R. Williams Parry:

Y dewraf o'n hawduron   (The bravest of our authors)

ELY

In section I (plot 246) of Western cemetery, about a quarter of a mile from the main entrance, lies **Walter Bartley Wilson** (1870?–1954), the prime mover in the formation of Cardiff City Football Club and its acceptance as a professional club in membership of the Second Division of the Southern League in 1910. Wilson, the club's first secretary, served briefly as its manager in 1933–4 and was still assistant secretary until shortly before his death. For many years his grave

remained unmarked, the headstone consigned to the undergrowth but, in 1999, it was found by a BBC film crew and restored to its rightful place with the inscription 'The Founder of Cardiff City AFC' added.

LLANDAFF

In the churchyard on the south side of Llandaff Cathedral, near the Lady chapel, is the tomb of the great architect **John Prichard** (1817–86). Son of the vicar of Llangan and a pupil of Pugin, he was responsible for the rebuilding and restoration of Llandaff Cathedral during the 1850s and many other churches in Cardiff and the Valleys (including St Margaret's, Roath, with its mausoleum to the Bute family). On the north side of the cathedral lie members of the Insole family of Llandaff, pioneers of the Cardiff coal trade. To **James Harvey Insole** (1821–1901) belongs the dubious distinction of being the owner of the notoriously unsafe Cymer colliery in the Rhondda, where, on 15 July 1856, there was an underground explosion which killed 114 miners, the worst mining disaster in Britain up to that time. Though he disclaimed any personal responsibility for the accident, he did pay for all the funerals.

Next to the churchyard is the main Llandaff cemetery, the resting place of **David Morgan** (1833–1919), founder of what is now one of Cardiff's largest shopping enterprises, having opened his drapers' shop at 23 The Hayes in 1879. Austere and thrifty to the point of obsession he insisted that every piece of paper, every length of string, every pin must be saved for future use. His approach to business was simple and straightforward: 'One price, plain figures, no discounts.' There was never a 'sale' in his establishment during his lifetime; he declined to humiliate his customers by implying that they were the sort of people who expected something for nothing. It is typical of the man that, as his biographer A. N. Morgan, his grandson, relates, he had the foresight to obtain in advance the bricks needed to line the vault of his grave, fearing a brick shortage during the war. The grave, headed by a handsome Celtic cross, may be found by following the main path curving from the cemetery entrance, turning right at the first crossroads, then right again at the next. Before the first turning right, beyond an archway of yew trees, is one of the most beautiful graves in the cemetery (row 37, grave 11), that of **Charles Philip Marment** and his two wives, **Jane**, who died in 1910, and **Constance**, who died in 1958. Charles himself died in 1942, at the age of eighty-six, after a lifetime in the high fashion business, first in Duke Street, then in Queen Street, Cardiff. His motto was 'the latest and best' and, a stylish dresser himself, he would parade through his store wearing a brown, black or grey bowler hat. Even at the age of eighty he would commute by train to Cardiff, four days a week, from his home in the Royal Crescent, Bath. Also buried in the cemetery is **Aneirin Talfan Davies** OBE (1909–80), the distinguished writer and broadcaster, who became Head of Programmes at BBC Wales from 1966 to 1969.

Charles Philip Marment, Llandaff

LLANISHEN

At the east end of St Isan's parish churchyard stands a rough granite headstone with the following inscription:

> Hier ruht
> unser liebes kind
> Helga Elisabeth Schoberth
> b. Nürnberg 5.10.33   d. Cardiff 13.12.37

(Here lies / our dear child / Helga Elisabeth Schoberth)

Helga, who died of meningitis, aged four, was the daughter of Dr Friedrich Schoberth, head of the German department at University College, Cardiff during the 1930s. According to John O'Sullivan (author of *A Century of Cardiff*, 2000), during the Second World War Schoberth acted as editor to William Joyce (Lord Haw Haw, who had himself lived in Cardiff before the war) and was believed by some to have been involved in the planning of air raids on Cardiff. When challenged about this in 1986 by O'Sullivan, Schoberth replied: 'How could I? My daughter is buried at Llanishen churchyard.'

PANTMAWR

Pantmawr cemetery is the resting place of the playwright and author **Jack Jones** CBE (1884–1970), probably best known for *Off to Philadelphia in the Morning* (1947), the biographical novel about the composer Joseph Parry. A few weeks before his death he received a Welsh Arts Council Award for his 'distinguished contribution to the literature of Wales'. He is buried in section D (plot number 462) on the right of the main entrance.

ROATH

The least distinguished of the Bute dynasty but the only one of the marquesses to be buried in Wales, the **1st Marquess of Bute** (1744–1814) is buried in St Margaret's church, Roath. James Boswell once described him as 'handsome, with elegant manners and a tempestuously noble soul, who never applied himself to anything'. However, he married well, first to Charlotte Windsor, thereby inheriting much land in and around Cardiff and, after her death, he married into the Coutts family, enhancing his fortune even more. Visitors to his tomb and those of his family members in the splendid Bute Mausoleum, redesigned in the 1880s, may well be struck by their resemblance to the tombs of the Russian tsars lying in the Peter and Paul fortress in St Petersburg. The seven massive sarcophagi, made of red Peterhead granite, certainly have no parallel in Britain, though the granite tombs of Napoleon III, Empress Eugénie and the Prince Imperial in Farnborough Abbey are similar.

ST FAGANS

Iorwerth Cyfeiliog Peate (1901–82), poet and pioneer of Welsh folk-life studies, was, like others nurtured in the radical hotbed of Llanbryn-mair, a man of strong opinions. A resolute pacifist, his conscientious objection during the Second World War briefly lost him his job in the National Museum of Wales until he was re-instated after a fierce campaign involving public figures such as Lloyd George and Aneurin Bevan. In 1948 he was appointed the first curator of the Welsh Folk Museum (now known as the Museum of Welsh Life). He retired in 1971 and after his death his ashes were buried behind the greatly admired eighteenth-century Unitarian chapel, Capel Pen-rhiw, from Drefach Felindre, Carms, which was re-erected at the museum in 1955.

THORNHILL

Wilfred Wooller (1912–97), one of Wales's twentieth-century sporting giants is buried in section R (plot number 152), to the left of the drive leading from the main entrance. Appropriately for someone who played eighteen times for Wales in the 1930s and captained Glamorgan when the team won the County Championship for the first time in 1948, his granite headstone bears the emblems of the Welsh Rugby Union and of Glamorgan County Cricket Club. In section H (plot number 1016), on the north side of the chapel lies **Frederick Charles Keenor** (1894–1972), the

greatest footballer ever to play for Cardiff City and the captain of the team which beat Arsenal 1–0 in the 1927 FA cup final at Wembley. He also played for Wales on thirty-two occasions. His grave, virtually covered by a thick carpet of grass, is almost impossible to find. In the next section eastwards, section G (plot number 2208) lie the ashes of a Welsh boxing hero, **Joe Erskine** (1934–90), British and Empire heavyweight champion from 1956 to 1958, 'gone but never forgotten'. Not far away (G 1566) are the ashes of **Arwel Hughes** (1909–88), Head of the Music Department of BBC Wales from 1965 to 1971 and composer of the tune to that great Welsh hymn 'Tydi a roddaist'. At the northernmost section of the cemetery (Aii plot number 2139) lie the cremated remains of the great Welsh actress **Rachel Thomas** (1905–95), the archetypal 'Welsh Mam'. She first came to prominence in the film *The Proud Valley* (1940), a sentimental, yet powerful drama featuring Paul Robeson, set in south Wales during the Depression. The film critic of *The Times*, C. A. Lejeune, referred to her as 'the symbol of all miners' wives and mothers'. She was even better as Beth Morgan in the BBC television version of Richard Llewellyn's *How Green Was My Valley*, and for nearly twenty years she played Bella in the popular Welsh soap opera *Pobol y Cwm*.

WHITCHURCH

Charles Burley Ward (1876–1921), a hero of the Boer War, was the last person to be decorated with the Victoria Cross by Queen Victoria before her death. His grave, marked by a characteristic white military headstone, lies about fifty yards beyond the west wall of St Mary's parish church.

CARMARTHENSHIRE

AMMANFORD

James Griffiths (1890–1975), nowadays one of Wales's forgotten heroes, is buried in a modest grave in the near left-hand corner of the cemetery behind Gellimanwydd chapel (also known as the Christian Temple). President of the South Wales Miners' Federation during the Depression years, he represented Llanelli as a Labour MP from 1936 until 1970. As Minister for National Insurance in Attlee's post-war administration he played a major role in the establishment of the Welfare State, and served as Secretary of State for the Colonies, 1950–1. From 1964 to 1966 he was the first Secretary of State for Wales, with a seat in the Cabinet. An influential advocate of political devolution for Wales, he is said to have persuaded Harold Wilson not to appoint George Thomas as Secretary of State for Wales in 1974 because of the harm it would do to the cause. James's brother **David Rees Griffiths** (1882–1953), the poet **Amanwy**, is also buried in the cemetery, as is the poet and teacher **Watkin Hezekiah Williams** (1844–1905), better known as **Watcyn Wyn**. Translator of the hymns of Sankey and Moody, he was a celebrated hymn-writer in his own right, including the still popular 'Rwy'n gweld o bell y dydd yn dod' (I see from afar the day approaching). He lies under a white cross towards the opposite corner of the cemetery from James Griffiths.

In the graveyard in front of Bethany chapel, their headstones facing each other, lie two other distinguished Nonconformist ministers and poets, **William Nantlais Williams** (1874–1959) and **John Thomas Jôb** (1867–1938), winner of the Chair at the National Eisteddfod on three occasions and the Crown once.

BLAEN-Y-COED

Blaen-y-coed cemetery

In Blaen-y-coed cemetery, up in the hills above Cynwyl Elfed, lie the ashes of **Howell Elfet Lewis** (1860–1953), **Elfed**, a celebrated *eisteddfodwr* (winner of the Crown twice and the Chair once) and widely regarded as the greatest Welsh hymn-writer since William Williams, Pantycelyn. His resting place, marked by a brown marble cross, is on the right of the path leading from the back of Blaen-y-coed chapel. Elfed's birthplace, a pretty whitewashed stone cottage in the nearby hamlet of Y Gangell, is preserved as a memorial to this distinguished man.

CAEO

John Johnes (1800–76), a prominent west Wales landowner and judge, was murdered at his home, Dolaucothi, by his disaffected Irish butler, **Henry Tremble**, in August 1876. After killing Johnes's dogs and attempting to kill his sister, Tremble shot himself. This incident caused a sensation, and Tremble, initially buried in Caeo churchyard, was dug up and left on the road outside, only to be interred nearby for a time before being reburied in the churchyard in an unmarked grave. By contrast, the Johnes family vault has a prominent position in the churchyard and, apart from John Johnes, contains the remains of **Sir James Hills-Johnes** (1833–1919) who, as plain James Hills, was awarded the Victoria Cross for gallantry during the siege of Delhi in 1857. He earned his place in the Johnes family vault by marrying John Johnes's daughter in 1882, changing his name to Hills-Johnes by royal licence in the following year.

CARMARTHEN

Sir Richard Steele (1672–1729), dramatist, politician (he was once expelled from the House of Commons for 'uttering seditious libels') and essayist, is best known as founder of the *Tatler* (1709) and the *Spectator* (1711) in collaboration with Joseph Addison. His connection with Carmarthen came through his marriage in 1707, to his second wife, Mary Scurlock of Tŷ Gwyn, Llangunnor, whom he met at his first wife's funeral. After Mary's death in 1718, and short of money, he went to live first in Llangunnor (there is a fulsome tribute to him inside the church) and later in the centre of Carmarthen in what is now the Ivy Bush Hotel. After his death he was buried in the Scurlock vault in St Peter's parish church, near the south wall, a far cry from Westminster Abbey where his second wife lay. Nevertheless, he made his final journey with due ceremony, his coffin being escorted to the church by night by twenty-four attendants carrying lighted torches. When the vault was uncovered in 1876 Steele's skeleton was found to be sporting a natty wig with a black bow. Also buried in the church (his body having been relocated from Greyfriars, Carmarthen) is **Sir Rhys ap Thomas** (1449– 1525), Wales's most influential magnate during the early Tudor period. Henry VII's greatest Welsh supporter, he was knighted after the battle of Bosworth Field and appointed Chamberlain of South Wales. The bards of the time described him as 'pinagl holl Cymru' (the pinnacle of all Wales). Henry VIII called him 'Father Rhys'.

Arthur William Haggar (1851–1925), the film pioneer and showman, famous for the 'Haggar Royal Electric Bioscope' and for establishing a string of cinemas in south Wales before the First World War is buried in the grave of his first wife (plot C 583) in Carmarthen town cemetery. Or at least that is what the newspapers of the time reported, for, oddly, the cemetery records do not show that such a burial took place, doubtless a clerical error.

CRUG-Y-BAR
This small village, noteworthy for having given its name to the tune (composer unknown) accompanying one of Wales's favourite hymns, David Charles's 'O fryniau Caersalem ceir gweled' (From Jerusalem's hills one can see), is also the final resting place of the eighteenth-century hymn-writer **Dafydd Jones o Gaeo** (1711–77). Through his frequent journeys into England as a drover (he was well known as far afield as Barnet and Maidstone) he learned the English language and was best known as the translator into Welsh of the hymns of Isaac Watts. Jones is buried inside Crug-y-bar chapel where he worshipped for many years, and there is a marble memorial to him in the cemetery.

DREFACH FELINDRE
The ashes of **Gwyn Alfred Williams** (1925–95), one of the most versatile and best-loved historians of his time, are buried in the garden of his home, Tŷ Dyffryn, in the small village of Drefach Felindre, not far from Newcastle Emlyn.

FERRYSIDE
Somewhere in St Ishmael's churchyard is the grave of the radical lawyer **Hugh Williams** (1796–1874), Chartist, a vigorous defender of those prosecuted as 'Rebecca' rioters (though he was not the leader of the movement), and brother-in-law of the great Liberal statesman Richard Cobden.

GLANAMAN

In an unmarked grave in the somewhat bleak Tabernacle cemetery lies **James Colton** (1860?–1936), miner and anarchist, whose main claim to fame is as the husband-of-convenience of the most celebrated anarchist of her day, Emma Goldman (1869–1940), branded 'the most dangerous woman in America' (Maureen Stapleton won an Oscar playing the part in Warren Beatty's film *Reds*).

Further up the hill, in a rather remote spot, is Hen Bethel cemetery, the resting place of one of Wales's greatest entertainers **Ryan Davies** (1937–77). His rendering of 'Myfanwy' on the recording 'Ryan at the Rank' is still regarded by some as the best version of this evergreen melody. His grave is on the right of the main path.

KIDWELLY

On the east wall of the churchyard, near to his grave, is a modern plaque commemorating **William Davies** (1784–1851), 'Welsh Methodist pioneer in west Wales and their first missionary abroad'. Within three years of arriving in Sierra Leone he had become mayor of Freetown only to return home in 1818 because of ill health. The malaria which had killed his first wife in Sierra Leone took a heavy toll on him too, affecting his mental health, and although he continued to minister for several years his increasingly odd behaviour forced his retirement in 1841. Ten years later, Davies was found hanged near his home in Kidwelly.

At the spot still known as Maes Gwenllïan, about a mile and a half from Kidwelly castle where she was executed, the great Welsh heroine **Gwenllïan** (*c*.1097–1136), dubbed the 'Second Queen of the Amazons' by Gerald of Wales, was defeated by the Normans. Presumably her remains are still somewhere in the area.

LAUGHARNE

'One, I am a Welshman; two, I am a drunkard; three, I am a lover of the human race, especially of women.' On the whole, the human race loved him in return. Certainly at the time of his death in New York, from chronic over-indulgence, **Dylan Thomas** (1914–53) was undoubtedly the most celebrated poet in the English-speaking world. He is still probably the world's best-known Welshman, acclaimed for his play for voices *Under Milk Wood*, and the poems 'Fern Hill' and especially 'Do Not Go Gentle into that Good Night'. His middle name 'Marlais' came from his great-uncle, Gwilym Marles, a heroic nineteenth-century Unitarian radical but probably not a man after Dylan's own heart. 'Land of my fathers? My fathers can keep it,' he once said. Dylan's grave, and that of his wife **Caitlin** (who died in 1994), is marked by a simple, but easy to spot, white wooden cross in the middle of the annexe to St Martin's parish churchyard.

LLANDDOWROR

There are many who regard Carmarthenshire's **Griffith Jones** (1683–1761) as the eighteenth century's most influential Welshman. A preacher of towering authority, his words led to the conversion of the great Daniel Rowland. Jones was also determined to make the Welsh people literate, especially the hitherto neglected poor and underprivileged, and in 1731 he established the Circulating Schools movement, which brought literacy of sorts to about half the population of Wales and came to the notice of people as far away as Catherine the Great of Russia. The movement also secured the vitality of the Welsh language. His greatest patron was **Madam Bridget Bevan** (1698–1779), a wealthy philanthropist from Laugharne who, after Jones's death, continued his work with great success. Following her own death in 1779 she was buried alongside Jones in the chancel of Llanddowror church.

LLANDOVERY

In Llanfair-ar-y-bryn churchyard, on the outskirts of the town, lies Wales's finest hymn-writer, **William Williams, Pantycelyn** (1717–91). His output was prodigious, comprising over 900 hymns, including such evergreens as 'Pererin wyf mewn anial dir' (I am a pilgrim in a desertland) – sung to the tune 'Amazing Grace' – and 'Arglwydd arwain trwy'r anialwch', best known in its English version 'Guide me, O Thou great Jehovah'. He once attributed his poetic gifts to:

> Enjoyment of God, and experience, together with the force of heavenly fervour, boiling together within, until the fire breaks forth in sweet songs that shall endure for ever.

He is still widely referred to by Welsh preachers as 'Y Pêr Caniedydd' (The Sweet Singer). A substantial obelisk marks his grave in the north-east of the churchyard.

Rhys Prichard (1579–1644), the 'Old Vicar' of Llandovery, was a different sort of chap altogether. He was, for many years, a hopeless drunkard who would spend most of his waking hours in the local hostelries until, according to George Borrow, 'he was generally trundled home in a wheelbarrow in a state of utter insensibility'. Having suddenly seen the error of his ways he took to writing popular verse aimed at ordinary people, combining religious exhortation and homely wisdom, which was collected together in book form after his death, with the title *Canwyll y Cymru* (the Welshmen's candle). This publication is said to have had as much impact in Wales as Bunyan's *Pilgrim's Progress* in England. After his death he was buried, according to the account in *Wild Wales*, in the churchyard at Llandingad though George Borrow reports that in the mid-eighteenth century 'his tomb was swept by a dreadful inundation of the river, which swept away not only tombs but dead bodies out of graves'. There is, however, a monument in his memory behind the church altar.

LLANDYBÏE
William Gilbert Anthony Parkhouse (1925–2000) is considered by many to have been the most stylish Welsh-born batsman to play for Glamorgan. A prolific run-scoring opener (he exceeded 1,000 runs in a season fifteen times) and a brilliant slip fielder, he played seven times for England in the 1950s and it should have been more. He was undoubtedly disadvantaged by playing for an unfashionable county side during an era when England was well blessed with high-quality opening batsmen. He could certainly consider himself unlucky to have been dropped for the Fifth Test against India in 1959 having shared an opening stand of 146 with Geoff Pullar at Headingley in the Third, then a first-wicket record for England against India. His ashes are buried in Llandybïe parish churchyard.

LLANDYFAELOG
On the right of the path leading up to the church door, under a restored chest tomb, lies **Peter Williams** (1723–96), one of the leaders of the early Methodist movement in Wales who was once locked in the kennels of the fiercely hostile Sir Watkin Williams Wynn for his pains. He produced an English translation of William Williams, Pantycelyn's great Welsh hymn including the famous first verse which opens with the words 'Guide me, O Thou great Jehovah', and in 1770 published a popular edition of the Welsh Bible (said to be the first version to be printed in Wales), with a

commentary after every chapter, and which sold in its thousands. His last years were embroiled with controversy when he was accused by his fellow Methodists of preaching heresy, an issue reflected in the rather bitter epitaph on his grave:

Underneath are deposited the remains of the Revd Peter Williams late of Gelliledinais in this parish. All his labours were invariably directed to promote the temporal and eternal welfare of his countrymen for whose benefit he published 3 Editions of a Welsh Bible with Explanatory Notes, one Edition in 8vo, a concordance and a number of pamphlets in the same language in return for which alas he experienced nothing but persecution and ingratitude. He continued a faithful and laborious minister of the Gospel for 53 years and died rejoicing in his God, August 8th 1796, aged 74 years.

LLANFIHANGEL-AR-ARTH
In the north-west corner of the churchyard lies 'the Welsh miracle girl', **Sarah Jacob** (1857–69). Her sad story, related by John Cule (*Wreath on the Crown*, 1967), illustrates the reservoir of latent medieval superstition persisting within Nonconformist Wales in the late 1860s, when thousands of curious visitors (including Dylan Thomas's great-uncle, Gwilym Marles) descended on Lletherneuadd, a remote farmhouse in the middle of rural Carmarthenshire, to gawp at a young girl who seemed to be surviving without eating or drinking anything. The likeliest explanation was that, possibly aided and abetted by her younger sister, Sarah, rather enjoying her celebrity status, was managing to feed herself surreptitiously but, once observed day and night by a team of nurses from Guy's Hospital she allowed herself to expire rather than admit her deception. Her naive parents, who apparently believed themselves to be in the presence of a veritable saint, were convicted of manslaughter and imprisoned. No action was taken against the doctors and nurses who stood by and watched as the tragedy unfolded.

LLANGUNNOR
Though nowadays largely forgotten **Sir Lewis Morris** (1833–1907), a Carmarthen lawyer, was, at the end of the nineteenth century, one of Britain's most popular poets, with his books selling in their tens of thousands. By 1896, 40,000 copies of his best-known work, *The Epic of Hades*, had been sold. On Tennyson's death in 1892 Morris aspired to the position of Poet Laureate, though doubts as to whether he was at the time married to the mother of his three

children seem to have counted against him. Lord Rosebery, who knew a lot more about horses than he did about poetry, awarded Morris a knighthood 'for services to literature' in 1895 as something of a consolation prize. When he died, he was buried in the churchyard, under a tree at the west end of the church, in accordance with a wish he had expressed many years earlier:

> Let me at last be laid
> On that hillside I know which scans the vale,
> Beneath the thick yews' shade
> For shelter when the rains and winds prevail.

Near the south wall of the church, under a recently renovated chest-tomb, lies **David Charles** (1762–1834), brother of Thomas Charles, and author of three of Wales's greatest hymns, 'O! Iesu mawr' (O! great Jesus) (Llef), 'O fryniau Caersalem' (From Jerusalem's hills) (Crug-y-bar) and 'Rhagluniaeth fawr y nef' (Great providence of heaven) (Builth).

LLANSTEFFAN

Glyn Jones (1905–95) is acknowledged as one of the greatest of Welsh writers in English through his poetry, plays and novels, and his book *The Dragon has Two Tongues*, published in 1968, a highly acclaimed review of Welsh writers in English, won a Welsh Arts Council prize in the following year. His ashes are buried in the churchyard of the village where many of his forebears lived, and the spot, near to the west door of the church, is marked by a simple plaque containing the word *Llenor* (man of letters).

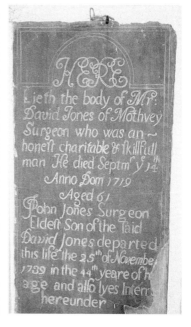

MYDDFAI

The 'Physicians of Myddfai', who made this isolated village a centre of research and healing long before the advent of modern medicine, date back to the thirteenth century when fact and myth combined in the person of the Lady of Llyn y Fan Fach. She was a fairy who passed to her sons, notably Rhiwallon, the first and most famous of the physicians, secret remedies for the cure of all manner of ills, thus beginning a tradition of healing by generations of physicians of Myddfai, much of it preserved in manuscript collections in some of the major British libraries. **David Jones** (*c*.1658–1719) and his son **John Jones** (*c*.1696– 1739) are believed to be the last of the line of the physicians of Myddfai. They are buried together in St Michael's churchyard and the stone which once covered their grave now stands just inside the church entrance. David Jones's epitaph commemorates 'an honest, charitable and skillful man'.

NEWCASTLE EMLYN
During the Rebecca riots in 1843, the 4th Light Dragoons were very much in evidence in Carmarthen, the centre of the agitation at the time. One of the troops involved in the charge on the Carmarthen workhouse in June 1843 was **John Kearns** (1818?– 43) who, a few days later, drowned while swimming in the river at Newcastle Emlyn. He was buried outside the wall of the tower at the west end of Holy Trinity church, and his untimely end was recorded on the headstone. Though the epitaph is now almost totally illegible it is, fortunately, quoted in Pat Molloy's book *And They Blessed Rebecca* (1983), and reads as follows:

He fell not in the battle strife, nor on the sultry plain.
Death did not meet the warrior there, nor on the stormy main.
But there, in Tivy's winding stream, one sunny summer's day,
Where bathing peacefully he sank, his spirit passed away.
Mourn reader, with his comrades mourn, o'er one so young and brave,
and trust in Him whose mighty arm from endless death can save.

Towards the top left-hand corner of the Gelli cemetery on the Cenarth Road out of Newcastle Emlyn is the simple grave of **Dr Martyn Lloyd-Jones** (1899–1981), 'the beloved Doctor'. He gave up a promising medical career in London to become what he later called 'a full-time preacher of the glorious gospel of the blessed God', first in south Wales, then as pastor of Westminster Chapel, London, from 1939 to 1968. He was generally acknowledged as the most powerful pulpit orator of his generation, though his uncompromising beliefs, rooted firmly in the Bible, and once described as seventeenth-century Puritanism, were uncomfortable to many in an age of ecumenism and liberalism.

RHYDCYMERAU
Buried in the small cemetery of the Calvinistic Methodist chapel, by the path, is the legendary Welsh patriot **David John Williams** (1885–1970), teacher, author of the classic *Hen Dŷ Ffarm* (1953) (translated into English by Waldo Williams as *The Old Farmhouse*), and a founder member of Plaid Cymru. He was one of the three celebrated arsonists of Penyberth (1936), though, typically of someone who, by nature and appearance, was the least likely of criminals, he managed to get his own matches wet, and it is said that he quite enjoyed his time in prison because of the characters he came across.

TALYLLYCHAU
Though most people accept that Dafydd ap Gwilym was buried at Strata Florida there is a determined minority, by no means deflected by the fact that Iolo Morganwg shared their view, who insist that Wales's greatest bard is buried in the churchyard at Talyllychau. In 1984 a headstone was erected at the east end of the churchyard at the spot assumed to be his resting place, with the supporting evidence inscribed upon it.

CEREDIGION

ABERARTH
Llanddewi Aberarth, past winner of the accolade 'Best Kept Churchyard in the Deanery of Glyn Aeron', contains the ashes of **Sir Geraint Evans** (1922–92), who, having graced the opera houses of the world for over thirty years, making the part of Figaro his own, retired to Aberaeron, where he became a part-time coastguard before dying of a heart attack. The Sir Geraint Evans Wales Heart Research Institute, built at the University of Wales College of Medicine following a major fund-raising initiative involving towns and villages throughout Wales, stands as a permanent memorial to one of Wales's greatest cultural ambassadors. The churchyard also contains the ashes of Sir Geraint's brother-in-law, **Glyn Davies** (1927–76), the richly talented rugby outside-half who played for Cambridge University, Pontypridd and Wales (ten caps) in the early post-war years.

ABERYSTWYTH

In the town cemetery, Llanbadarn Road, lie some of Wales's greatest cultural heroes, probably first and foremost being **David James Jones** (1899–1968), **Gwenallt**, widely regarded as one of the finest poets in the Welsh language of the twentieth century. He had the unique ability to express in elegant, evocative, sometimes angry, often poignant verse some of the recurring themes of Welsh life,

Christianity and the challenge of socialism ('There is a place for the fist of Karl Marx in His Church'), and industrial deprivation. No Welsh poet has been more quoted from the pulpit during the last fifty years. Gwenallt's unmistakeable grave (section 2, number 212), topped by a solid slab of Welsh slate, lies on the eastern side of the cemetery, not far from its northern perimeter, on the right of the main path. A few yards away (section 2, number 109) is the grave of his university teacher, **Thomas Gwynn Jones** (1871–1949), for nearly twenty years professor of Welsh literature at the University College of Wales, Aberystwyth, and considered the most gifted Welsh literary figure of the first half of the twentieth century. He won the Chair at the National Eisteddfod twice, and the ode on the first occasion in 1902, 'Ymadawiad Arthur' (The Passing of Arthur), is regarded as a work of genius which established a new epoch in Welsh poetry. He was a distinguished folklorist, biographer, translator, literary critic and travel writer, and probably deserved more than the CBE he received in 1937. To those who expressed surprise that he was willing to accept anything at all, bearing in mind his socialist and pacifist past ('a pacifist with the emphasis on the fist', he once said), he confessed that he was no longer the hothead he once had been. A little way southwards (section 2, number 435) can be seen a commanding brown marble obelisk marking the grave of the **Reverend Thomas Levi** (1825–1916), a man of many parts, who established in 1862 and edited for nearly fifty years the phenomenally popular monthly magazine *Trysorfa y Plant* which, in its heyday in the 1880s achieved a monthly circulation of 45,000. An essentially devotional, certainly 'improving' magazine, particularly aimed at young people, it provided an early platform for some of the great writers of the period. His son **Thomas Arthur Levi**

(1874–1954), the colourful professor of law at Aberystwyth, is buried in the same grave. A little further south (section 3, number 801) lies **Sir John Williams** (1840– 1926), royal physician and the guiding force in the establishment of the National Library of Wales, donating his priceless and unique collection of Welsh books and manuscripts to the venture, provided it was located in Aberystwyth. A proud Welshman, he was also instrumental in having Wales identified separately rather than under 'England and Wales' in the *Medical Directory*.

In the north-western section of the cemetery, not far from each other, lie two other knights of the realm. **Sir Harold Idris Bell** (1879–1967), one time Keeper of Manuscripts and Egerton Librarian at the British Museum, was the distinguished translator into English of Thomas Parry's *Hanes Llenyddiaeth Gymraeg hyd 1900* (1945) under the title *A History of Welsh Literature* (1955), adding an excellent concluding section of his own on the twentieth century. **Sir John Gibson** (1841–1915), was the formidable editor of the *Cambrian News* from 1873 until his death. He was a combative man of strong opinions. Thomas Jones, Lloyd George's private secretary, once wrote that 'every public man in the counties of Cardigan and Merioneth lived in fear of being dipped in his inkpot'. The headstone on his grave (section 2, number 261) carries the following remarkable epitaph:

> He took such cognisance of men and things
> If any beat a horse you felt he saw;
> If any cursed a woman he took note;
> Yet stared at nobody; you stared at him,
> And found, less to your pleasure than surprise,
> He seemed to know you and expect as much.
> So, next time that a neighbour's tongue was loosed,
> It marked the shameful and notorious fact,
> We had among us, not so much a spy,
> As a recording chief-inquisitor,
> The town's true master, if the town but knew;
> We merrily kept a governor for form,
> While the man walked about and took account
> Of all thought, said and acted, then went home
> And wrote it fully to our Lord the King.

LLANBADARN FAWR

Inside the historic church of St Padarn, referred to in the poems of Dafydd ap Gwilym, and where Bishop William Morgan started his

NEAR THIS PLACE LIE
THE MORTAL REMAINS OF
LEWIS MORRIS
LLYWELYN DDU O'FÔN
SCHOLAR·PHILOSOPHER·POET·PATRIOT·
BORN AT PENTREFEIRIANELL·ANGLESEY
MARCH 2ⁿᵈ 1700.
DIED AT PENBRYN IN THIS COUNTY
APRIL 11ᵀᴴ 1765.
THIS MEMORIAL WAS PLACED HERE
TO MARK A SPOT DEAR TO WALES
BY HIS GREAT-GRANDSON
LEWIS MORRIS
AD 1884.

"AC YN HEWYROD Y CYFIAWR. CARR"
"AC YN HOHARD. CARU POB HANFOD"
"AC YN HCHARU POB HANFOD, CARU DUW"

Lewis Morris (1700 [sic]–1765),
Llanbadarn Fawr

ministry, lies **Lewis Morris** (1701–65), the greatest member of one of the most remarkable families of eighteenth-century Wales. A fervent patriot, he strove to defend the literary heritage and language of Wales in the face of encroaching Anglicization. He was an assiduous patron of some of the leading figures of the time (including Goronwy Owen and Ieuan Fardd), and was the hub of the so-called 'Morris Circle' of Welsh poets and scholars. With his brother he established the Honourable Society of Cymmrodorion in 1751. On the floor of the nave is a memorial to Morris by the nineteenth-century poet Sir Lewis Morris:

> Near this spot lie the mortal remains of Lewis Morris (Llewelyn Ddu o Fôn), Scholailosopher, Poet, Patriot . . . This memorial was placed here to mark a spot dear to Wales by his great-grandson.

Nearby is the Gogerddan vault, the resting place of the **Pryses of Gogerddan**, one of the great landed families of west Wales for over 300 years. Among the more colourful members of the family was **Sir Edward Pryse** (1862–1918) who, as Master of the Tivyside Hunt, caused a scandal following the death of Queen Victoria in January 1901. While the whole nation was supposed to be in mourning Pryse and his companions continued to hunt. The local paper carried several hard-hitting verses written by a 'Loyal and Disgusted Sportsman' (quoted in H. M. Vaughan's *The South Wales Squires*, 1926), the first verse reading as follows:

> Master Pryse to his Hunt said, I'm foolish and blunt,
> Times are bad, but my grief I can stay,
> And I don't care a jot, if you feel it or not,
> For I mean to go hunting today.

Pryse served in the Welsh Regiment during the First World War, earning the Ordre du Mérite Agricole from the French government in recognition of his contribution to the prevention of damage to land and crops during the course of hostilities. Also buried in the church are two brothers who, born in Aberystwyth and educated at Oxford, both went on to pursue distinguished legal careers in India. **Lewis Pugh Pugh** (1837–1908), Liberal MP for Cardiganshire 1880–5, was in fact born 'Evans' but changed his name to Pugh to inherit his bachelor uncle's substantial Aber-mad estate. During his time in India he became Advocate General of Bengal and a member of the Governor General's Council. At the time of his death the *Calcutta Statesman* reported that:

> professionally and socially Mr Pugh has been a prominent figure in Calcutta for a period beyond the memory of all save the few who survive him, and never made one enemy. His death is one more reminder that the age of giants has passed away and the day of mediocrity dawned.

Sir Griffith Humphrey Pugh Evans (1840–1902) served on the Viceroy's Legislative Council and became a Knight Commander of the Indian Empire in 1892. There is a memorial to the two brothers in Calcutta Cathedral, stating that they are buried in Llanbadarn Fawr, probably the only Welsh graves advertised in India. Some Welsh people never returned and lie, largely forgotten, in some desolate Indian graveyard. One such was the Reverend Thomas Jones (1810–49), the Montgomeryshire man who took Welsh Calvinistic Methodism to the people of the Khasi Hills, in north-east India, and who is still revered in that part of the world. He now lies in the Scottish cemetery, Calcutta, 'overshadowed by palms and circled by vultures and huge black kites', in the words of Nigel Jenkins (*Gwalia in Khasia*, 1995).

Outside, by the east wall of the church, lies **George Ernest John Powell** (1842–82), the bohemian squire of Nanteos who was a friend of the poet Algernon Swinburne, with whom he would roister in the streets of Aberystwyth. Powell hated the country pursuits of his class and, when once given a gun by his father and told to go out and shoot something, proceeded to shoot one of Colonel Powell's prize bullocks.

LLANDDEWIBREFI

In the parish cemetery lies the traveller and writer **Jonathan Ceredig Davies** (1859–1932), whose full and varied life is described on his headstone. For many years he lived in Patagonia, then

Western Australia, where he observed and later wrote about the lives and customs of the colonists. On his return to Wales he also wrote a well-informed book about the *Folklore of West and Mid-Wales* and, when an old man, he painstakingly wrote, and printed himself, page after tiring page, a 500-page book of reminiscences, for, as he said in the preface, 'I do not believe in being idle'.

Set into the north-west corner wall of St David's church is a fragment of a gravestone dating from the seventh century which, when brought to light by the great antiquary, Edward Lhuyd, in 1693, had carried the following inscription, quoted by R. J. Collier in his book *The Teifi – Scenery and Antiquities of a Welsh River* (1987):

Hic jacet Idnert, filius Jacobi qui occisus fuit propter predam santi david

(Here lies Idnert, son of Jacob who was killed on account of the plunder of David's sanctuary)

Most of the wording has now been obscured but this inscription is regarded as the earliest written reference to the patron saint of Wales in existence.

LLANDYFRIOG
In the churchyard, on the right of the main path, not far from the entrance, stands a rather chunky obelisk marking the grave of **David Emlyn Evans** (1843–1913), probably the leading Welsh music critic of his day, even though he never wholly shared the adulation felt by most of his countrymen for Joseph Parry whom he regarded as too much of a self-publicist. Evans was also a prolific composer of melodies, both secular and sacred. They included two hymn tunes still popular today, 'Eirinwg' and 'Trewen', the first few bars of which are carved at the foot of his memorial. On the other side of the church, not far from the west wall, is the grave of **Thomas Heslop** (1780–1814), shot dead by John Beynon in what is said to be the last recorded duel to have taken place in Wales. Apparently the incident followed an argument in the Salutation Inn, Newcastle Emlyn, over the moral rectitude of the barmaid. The slab of slate covering his resting place carries the poignant epitaph: 'Alas poor Heslop'. Though convicted of manslaughter, Beynon, who had influential friends, was set free but, confronted by local hostility, he fled to America.

LLANGEITHO
Inside the church is the resting place of **Daniel Rowland** (1713–90)

who, though for much of his life an Anglican curate, was the greatest preacher of the Welsh Methodist revival. Llangeitho, a remote community in deepest Cardiganshire, became the 'Mecca' to which thousands were attracted from all over Wales to be driven into a frenzy by Rowland's vivid descriptions of hell. As William Williams, Pantycelyn was to relate:

> Terror, amazement, fear caught the people, great and small, every face lost its colour, knees trembled with the thunder as if death itself had taken possession of everyone in the crowd, and the cry 'What shall we do to save our souls?' arose from every side.

LLANGRANNOG

An elegant obelisk and urn of black marble mark the grave of the remarkable **Sarah Jane Rees** (1839–1916), better known as **Cranogwen**, above Llangrannog church, at the point where hill side and churchyard merge into each other. An independent woman, she chose not to conform to the conventional female role of wife and mother, preferring to qualify as a merchant mariner like her father, becoming acknowledged as the best navigation instructor in Wales. She was a popular preacher with the Calvinistic Methodists, despite the reluctance of some ministers and elders to see her standing in the pulpit, and she won the poetry competition at the 1865 National Eisteddfod. From 1879 to 1892 she edited a new Welsh magazine for women, *Y Frythones* (The British woman), and, a lifelong campaigner against the 'demon drink', she spent her later years promoting temperance among the women of south Wales.

Cranogwen, Llangrannog

LLEDROD

Evan Evans (1731–88), known by the names **Ieuan Brydydd Hir** and more commonly **Ieuan Fardd**, spent much of his adult life as a frustrated curate. However, he is regarded by authorities such as Sir Thomas Parry as the greatest scholar of the eighteenth century, and his book *Some Specimens of the Poetry of the Ancient Welsh Bards*

(1764) brought the literature of the Welsh medieval poets to the attention of English scholars. In his writings he also sought to arouse a sense of national pride among his compatriots, many of whom he criticized for embracing too readily the culture of the English gentry. Unfortunately he was himself by no means perfect for, as Dr Samuel Johnson was to observe in his *Journey into North Wales in the Year 1774*, Evans was 'incorrigibly addicted to strong drink' and he spent the last years of his life in straitened circumstances, living mainly on charity in his native village of Lledrod. According to his biographer Daniel Silvan Evans, he is buried in the churchyard in an unmarked grave within the iron railings surrounding the grave of the Hughes family of Cwm Llechwedd.

LLWYNRHYDOWEN

In the centre of the village stands the old Unitarian chapel where **William Thomas**, better known as **Gwilym Marles** (1834–79), the radical champion of political and religious freedom (and great-uncle of Dylan Thomas), was pastor from 1860 to 1876, and where **Mary**, his first wife, was buried. On a headstone outside the main door is a warm tribute to her memory:

> Not learned, save in gracious household ways,
> Not perfect, nay, but full of tender wants;
> No angel, but a dearer being, all dipt
> In angel instincts, breathing Paradise.

In 1876 in a national cause célèbre, Marles and his congregation were evicted from their chapel by a vindictive anti-Liberal landowner, and a nationwide appeal fund enabled a new chapel to be built just along the road towards Talgarreg. He died shortly after the opening of the chapel and is buried near to the main door.

NEW CROSS

At the top of Horeb chapel cemetery is the rather neglected grave of **Caradoc Evans** (1878–1945), one of the most controversial Welsh writers of the twentieth century, whose works betrayed a truly pathological revulsion for organized Welsh Nonconformity. It is claimed that he coined the now common expression 'big-heads' to describe the deacons and the other self-important leaders of the Nonconformist chapels. He certainly revelled in his reputation as 'the most hated man in Wales' and the appearance of his collection of short stories, *My People*, in 1915 caused a sensation. While

English critics on the whole hailed the book as a work of real literary merit, most Welsh people hated it because it made them look stupid. He composed this tender inscription for his gravestone:

> Bury me lightly so that the small rain
> may reach my face, and the fluttering
> of the butterfly shall not escape my ear.

PENBRYN

Penbryn church, near Tre-saith, is a wonderfully atmospheric place, remote and perched high above the Ceredigion coast. At the top of the churchyard, under a substantial brown marble cross, lies **Anne Adaliza Puddicombe**, better known as **Allen Raine** (1836–1908) who, at the beginning of the twentieth century, was one of the best-selling authors of the day. Her most popular novel, *A Welsh Singer* (1897), had sold over 300,000 copies by the time of her death and in 1915 a silent film version appeared with Edith Evans making her screen debut. In the first volume of his autobiography Emlyn Williams recalled the powerful impact that novel made on an impressionable seven-year-old mind.

SILIAN

On the left-hand side of the eastern section of Silian churchyard, near Lampeter, about eighty yards from the back of the church, lies **Julian Cayo-Evans** (1937–95), breeder of palomino stallions and leader of the Free Wales Army during the 1960s. Although never as threatening as they liked to make out, nine of the ringleaders were rounded up by a nervous government in the build-up to the investiture of Prince Charles in 1969 and, on the very day of the investiture, six were convicted of various public order offences, three being jailed. Julian Cayo-Evans received the longest sentence, fifteen months' imprisonment. After his release he returned to farming.

STRATA FLORIDA

Dafydd ap Gwilym (*c.*1320–70) is generally regarded as Wales's greatest ever poet, touching the eternal themes of love and the beauty of nature. A member of a noble family, Dafydd was probably born at Brogynin, near Llanbadarn. Otherwise not much is known about his life, though he did travel about Wales, as his poetry shows. It is generally accepted that he was buried near a yew tree at Strata Florida abbey, where there is a commemorative plaque, though there is another tradition that locates his burial place at Talyllychau abbey. **Sir David James** (1887–1967) is certainly buried at Strata Florida, near the abbey wall. A native of Pontrhydfendigaid, he was a wealthy philanthropist who lavished money on many good causes in Wales, religious and cultural, including the Urdd and the National Eisteddfod. His substantial memorial refers to 'a good man, noble of character, and fully worthy of the praise given him'. Others buried in Strata Florida include **Gruffudd**, **Maelgwn** and **Hywel Sais**, sons of the twelfth-century Rhys ap Gruffudd (the Lord Rhys), and a tramp who had once been a soldier during the Afghan Wars of the 1880s. His frozen body was found on the snow-covered hills of Cardiganshire in February 1929, with fourpence ha'penny, a copy of *Old Moore's Almanack* and a photograph of a young girl in his pocket. The local people paid for his gravestone, on which is written:

> He died upon the hillside drear
> Alone, where snow was deep.
> By strangers he was carried here
> Where princes also sleep.

Undoubtedly the oddest headstone in the cemetery, near the grave of Dafydd ap Gwilym, commemorates the amputated **left leg of Henry Hughes** – the rest of him managed to emigrate to America. The headstone, which bears an outline of the member in question, carries the following inscription:

> The left leg and part
> Of the Thigh of Henry
> Hughes Cooper was cut
> off & interr'd here June
> the 18th 1756

An amusing poem by John Ormond, 'Lament for a Leg', which at one point, inevitably, refers to 'one foot in the grave', is included in R. Garlick and R. Mathias (eds), *Anglo-Welsh Poetry 1480–1980* (1984).

TALGARREG
The village of Talgarreg was the last home of the great Welsh poet **David Emrys James** (1881–1952) who, under his bardic name **Dewi Emrys**, won the Chair at the National Eisteddfod of 1926 and the

Crown on four occasions, 1929, 1930, 1943 and 1948. After his fourth success at Bridgend the rules were changed so that henceforth no one could win either the Chair or the Crown more than twice. He is buried in the chapel cemetery at Pisgah, about half a mile up the hill from Talgarreg. The prominent stone memorial can be seen straight ahead from the cemetery entrance, about thirty yards away. The headstone carries a couplet composed by the poet himself:

Melys hedd wedi aml siom   (Sweet peace after many
Distawrwydd wedi storom.   disappointments
                                  Quiet after the storm.)

TREGARON

Under a solid chest-tomb just outside the west door of St Caron's church lies **Ebenezer Richard** (1781–1837), an important figure in the development of Calvinistic Methodism in mid and south Wales and instrumental in drawing up the denomination's confession of faith in 1823. However his chief claim to fame must be as the father of Henry Richard, the revered 'Apostle of Peace', who is himself buried in that Nonconformist Valhalla in north London, Abney Park cemetery. Also buried in Tregaron churchyard is one **Morgan George**, who died in 1837 aged fifteen. Versions of his epitaph may be seen all over the country:

Thus thus it is we all must tread
The gloomy regions of the dead.
No bloom of youth nor age can save
Our mortal bodies from the grave.

In the Calvinistic Methodist chapel cemetery, on the right-hand side, is the grave of **Nan Davies** (1910–70), who progressed from being secretary to the legendary radio producer, Sam Jones, to becoming a prizewinning producer herself with BBC Wales.

CONWY

COLWYN BAY

The crematorium was journey's end for two celebrated peace campaigners. **Bertrand Russell** (1872–1970), the philosopher and Campaign for Nuclear Disarmament activist, lived near Penrhyndeudraeth for many years before his death. At his request his cremation was conducted with absolutely no ceremony and his ashes were subsequently scattered. **Lewis Valentine** (1893–1986), first president of Plaid Genedlaethol Cymru (the Nationalist Party of Wales) in 1925, the party's first parliamentary candidate and one of the three Penyberth arsonists, enjoyed a distinguished career in the Baptist ministry. He was the author of 'Gweddi dros Gymru' which, sung to the tune 'Finlandia', is widely regarded as Wales's alternative national anthem. He spent his retirement years in Rhos-on-Sea and after his death he was cremated, though what happened to his ashes has never been publicly revealed.

CONWY

In the town cemetery lies **Samuel Roberts** (1800–85), one of Wales's leading nineteenth-century radicals, known to all as **SR**. Born in the chapel house of the celebrated Hen Gapel, Llanbrynmair and for some time the Independent minister there, he took a fiercely individualist approach to everything, opposing the Corn Laws, the power of the state in Church and education, and trade unionism in the name of freedom, and using his monthly journal *Y Cronicl* as a powerful platform for his views. His condemnation of landlordism, which enslaved the hard-working farmers of his native land, drove him to America in 1857, where he tried and failed to establish a Welsh settlement in Tennessee. He was a lifelong pacifist who denounced not only the Crimean War but even the American Civil War, making him unpopular with everyone, and he returned to Wales in 1867, to live in Conwy for the rest of his life.

DOLWYDDELAN

High above the village in the cemetery is the grave of **George Maitland Lloyd Davies** (1880–1949). The grandson of the celebrated Welsh preacher, John Jones, Talsarn, and for some years a Calvinistic Methodist minister himself, Davies was a pacifist of the purest sort, being a conscientious objector not only during the First, but also during the Second World War. Largely because of a split

Liberal vote in the 1923 general election he briefly, and most unexpectedly, became the Christian Pacifist MP for the University of Wales. The intensity of his immense moral courage took an increasingly heavy toll on him and he eventually committed suicide at the North Wales Mental Hospital a few days before Christmas 1949. Announcing his tragic death the *Western Mail* mourned him as 'one of the greatest Welshmen of his generation'. The stone on his grave, immediately to the right of the cemetery gate, three rows in, bears the simple epitaph 'Heddychwr' (peacemaker).

LLANEFYDD

Somewhere in the church of this small village, five miles north-west of Denbigh, lies **Catrin o Ferain** (1534/5–91), the most celebrated Welsh woman of the sixteenth century. Because of her several marriages to some of the leading members of Welsh society, Catrin came to be known as 'Mam Cymru', the 'Mother of Wales'. Among her most famous descendants were the Williams Wynn dynasty of Wynnstay and Hester Lynch Salusbury, wife of Henry Thrale. Legend has it that she used to have a string of lovers whom, when finished with, she would eliminate by pouring molten lead into their ears before burying them in the orchard of her estate.

LLANRWST

It is generally accepted that the stone coffin located in Gwydir chapel once held the body of the greatest of all the Welsh rulers of medieval Wales, **Llywelyn ap Iorwerth** (*c.*1173–1240) though what ultimately became of his body after his death at Aberconwy is not known.

At the top of St Mary's churchyard lies an authentic seventh son of a seventh son, the eccentric printer and bookseller **William John Roberts** (1828–1904). Universally known by his bardic name **Gwilym Cowlyd**, disenchanted by what he regarded as the debasement of the National Eisteddfod, he established in 1865 a rival, 'purer', movement known as Arwest Glan Geirionnydd, enjoying, he asserted, the special blessing of the Almighty himself. Proclaiming himself 'Chief Bard Positive of the Institutional Bards of the Isle of Britain', Gwilym held annual eisteddfodau by lake Geirionnydd, above Trefriw. Successful at first, they lost their impetus in later years and did not long survive his impoverished death. Nevertheless, towards the end of his life Gwilym was to proclaim his vision of presiding, as Chief Bard Positive, over a great Gorsedd of Peace, attended by all the crowned heads of the world, a prospect which evoked the following reaction from the *Illustrated London News*, quoted by Ivor Wynne Jones in his book *Minstrels and Miners* (1986):

> Gwilym from his Cymric Heights
> The great Mikado now invites
> To be his friend and brother.
> And, never wearying in his task
> Of making peace, proceeds to ask
> The Tzar to be another.
> More power then, Gwilym to thy lyre;
> May'st thou obtain thy heart's desire
> And from their follies wean them;
> When at the Eisteddfod they meet,
> May these two emperors compete,
> And share first prize between them.

TREFRIW

In a railed chest-tomb dominating St Mary's churchyard lies Gwilym Cowlyd's uncle, the clergyman **Evan Evans** (1795–1855) generally known as **Ieuan Glan Geirionnydd**, one of Wales's greatest nineteenth-century poets and hymn-writers. The English translation of a verse of one of his best-known poems, 'Ysgoldy Rhad Llanrwst' (the Llanrwst free school, where he went as a boy), reads as follows:

> The school bell is silent,
> No children attend any more from the town,
> And the bolts of the sturdy doors
> Rust where they stand.
> The bats in their silent flight
> Weave their drowsy way,
> Where once were recited
> The sweet works of Homer and Virgil.

Nowadays his most popular hymn is probably 'Ar lan Iorddonen ddofn' (On the banks of the deep Jordan) sung to Ieuan Gwyllt's tune 'Moab'.

DENBIGHSHIRE

BODELWYDDAN

In the churchyard of St Margaret's church ('the Marble Church') are 117 war graves marking the resting places of 34 British and

83 Canadian soldiers. Until the 1970s there was an army camp nearby, and the rumours were that the Canadian graves represented the sad aftermath of a riot by Canadian soldiers in 1919, followed by court martial and execution for mutiny. In fact, most of the soldiers died of natural causes, particularly influenza which was virulent at the time. There was indeed a riot among several hundred neglected Canadian soldiers, frustrated by the delay in their repatriation after the war, and five were killed in the skirmish, though it proved impossible to attribute any of the deaths to particular individuals. The headstone over **Corporal Joseph Young**'s grave (he died of bayonet wounds) bears the poignant epitaph 'Sometime, sometime, we'll understand'. The grave of **David Gillan**, who, according to the inscription 'was killed at Kinmel Park on March 5th 1919 defending the honour of his country' is, uniquely, marked by a cross. He was probably killed by his own side by mistake. In the north-east corner of the churchyard, by one of the floodlights, lies **Elizabeth Jones** (1822–86). In 1860 she married Robert Jones, a local publican and already father of two of her four children but, in 1842, as Elizabeth Parry, she had already given birth to the illegitimate John Rowlands, who spent his early years in the St Asaph workhouse before eventually becoming Sir Henry Morton Stanley, the eminent explorer.

DENBIGH

About halfway down on the right-hand side of the municipal cemetery is a simple slate headstone bearing the name **Catherine Williams**, better known as **Kate Roberts** (1891–1985), Wales's greatest prose writer of the twentieth century in the Welsh language. Her short stories were deeply rooted in the tightly knit Welsh-speaking communities of Caernarfonshire where she grew up, and dealt, with great sensitivity and eye for detail, with the central theme of much of her work, the struggle against poverty. Ardent Welsh Nationalists, she and her husband ran the radical Welsh-language newspaper *Baner ac Amserau Cymru* (The Banner and Times of Wales), also known as *Y Faner*, for two decades during which it became a vehicle for the writings of prominent members of Plaid Cymru, including Saunders Lewis and herself. Not far from her grave is the rather more elaborate pedestal memorial to the great publisher and propagandist **Thomas Gee** (1815–98), the founder of *Y Faner* (The Banner) in 1859, a publication which, by the time of his death had achieved a weekly circulation of 50,000.

He was a major force in the radical politics of nineteenth-century Wales, particularly championing the cause of the Welsh tenant-farmers.

In the churchyard of St Marcella's Church, Eglwyswen, lies **Thomas Edwards** (1739–1810), **Twm o'r Nant**, a struggling labourer for all his life but regarded by some as Wales's greatest eighteenth-century dramatist, particularly hailed for his interludes (*anterliwtiau*). Interludes were a form of drama much enjoyed by the ordinary people, performed by itinerant actors, usually in the open air with a wagon for a stage. Delivered in earthy, even bawdy, Welsh, the plays satirized members of the upper and middle classes who made the lives of the labouring poor so irksome – rapacious landlords, dissolute clerics, corrupt lawyers and the rest. While the targets of Twm's dramas found them offensive the audiences loved them and he was widely celebrated in his day as the 'Cambrian Shakespeare'. In *Wild Wales* (1862), George Borrow wrote an affectionate account of the colourful life of the man he called 'Tom o' the Dingle'. His grave, which is well marked, lies a little to the left of the path leading to the church door. Inside the church is the tomb of the celebrated antiquary **Humphrey Lhuyd** (1527–68) who drew the first map specifically of Wales, being published in Antwerp in 1573 as an appendix to Abraham Ortelius's atlas. Though not perfectly to scale the map was regularly reprinted until 1741.

LLANELIDAN

John Jones of Llanfor, known as **Coch Bach y Bala** (the little redhead from Bala) (1854–1913), was one of the best-known criminals of his age, not because he ever stole much of value but because, beginning in 1872 when he was jailed for four months after stealing an empty purse and a little knife, he spent the rest of his life constantly in and out of jail. His ability to escape from custody caught the public imagination at the time, and among his nicknames were the 'Welsh Houdini' and the 'little Welsh terror'. Having escaped from Ruthin jail in 1913 he was shot by the son of a local squire and died of his wound. Prior to the burial a local photographer took a picture of Jones in his coffin and sold hundreds of copies to the public. Fifty years after his death, and to the disgust of some, a commemorative stone was erected at his grave, to the south-east of St Elidan's church, to be found by taking the path leading from the main gate of the churchyard.

LLANGOLLEN

In the south-west of St Collen's churchyard stands an elaborately inscribed triangular tombstone marking the resting place of **Lady Eleanor Butler** (1739–1829) and the **Hon. Sarah Ponsonby** (1755–1831), the celebrated **Ladies of Llangollen**. These two aristocratic ladies eloped from Ireland in 1778 and settled at Plas Newydd, Llangollen, where they became a legend in their own lifetime. Many of the leading figures of the day came to see them – Castlereagh and Wellington, Sir Walter Scott, Robert Southey. William Wordsworth wrote a sonnet to the devoted pair in the garden of Plas Newydd, which referred to:

> Sisters in love, a love allowed to climb
> Ev'n on this earth, above the reach of time.

Buried with them is their faithful servant **Mary Carryll**, who had died in 1809 after a lifetime of loyal service for which she had received no payment other than any tips she might have picked up from the visitors.

Llandysilio churchyard, near to Llangollen, is the burial place of **Sir George Osborne Morgan** (1826–97), Liberal MP for Denbighshire from 1868 to 1897 and once described by Sir William Harcourt as one of the biggest bores in the House of Commons. However, as Judge Advocate General in Gladstone's second Liberal government, he piloted the 1880 Burial Act through the House of Commons, thereby enabling Nonconformists to be buried in parish churchyards in accordance with their own forms of service. It was a cause célèbre over the implementation of the Act in Llanfrothen in 1888 that first brought Lloyd George to public attention. During the same administration Morgan was responsible for the abolition of flogging in the British Army. His grave, on the right of the path from the church gate, is marked by an attractive Celtic cross.

LLANRHAEADR-YNG-NGHINMEIRCH

In the west of St Dyfnog's churchyard is the grave of **Ann Parry**

(1718?–87), a devout Methodist who, she said, was told by God that when she died her body would be as incorruptible as her soul. When her grave was opened in 1830 in order to accommodate her son it was found that her body, and indeed the flowers placed in her grave, were perfectly preserved. Three years later, when her son's wife was also laid to rest in the grave, Ann Parry's body was found to be in the same excellent condition as before. There were apparently many contemporary witnesses to this strange phenomenon. Her original headstone has, in recent years, been replaced by another carrying the inscription 'Fe wirodd Duw Ei Air' (God kept His Word).

NANTGLYN

The south side of St James's churchyard contains the grave of **William Owen Pughe** (1759–1835), friend of Iolo Morganwg and a truly eccentric character. Determined to demonstrate that there was something special about the Welsh, he concocted all manner of ostensibly scholarly but essentially spurious works to prove his point, such as his bardic alphabet (*Coelbren y Beirdd*), his *Cambrian Biography* and a Welsh–English dictionary twice as long as Johnson's English dictionary and full of fabrications. He is credited with coining the well-known cliché that Welsh is 'the language of heaven'. He was one of the twenty-four elders of the bizarre prophetess Joanna Southcott, who claimed, wrongly as it turned out, that she was carrying the New Messiah. Robert Southey referred to Owen Pughe as 'that good, simple-hearted Welsh-headed man' but also regarded him as the muddiest-minded man that he had ever met.

RHEWL

Robert Ambrose Jones (1851–1906), better known as **Emrys ap Iwan**, a Calvinistic Methodist minister in the Vale of Clwyd, was a passionate defender of Welsh nationhood and culture in the face of what he regarded as creeping Anglicization, and has been the inspiration of generations of Welsh-language activists since his death. He regarded the preservation of the Welsh language, pervading all aspects of the life and work of the people of Wales, as the only salvation of the nation.

> The Welsh language is the only defence between us and annihilation, and he who breaks down this defence by speaking the language of his conqueror without necessity and without cause is guilty of that negligence which shows a total lack of self-respect; and when a man ceases to respect himself, that man has, to all intents, ceased to be·

His grave, marked by a brown marble pedestal topped by an urn, stands prominently about halfway down the Calvinistic Methodist chapel cemetery.

RHYL

The man born **Robert Scourfield Mills** had several names during his lifetime, two of which are recorded on two separate headstones on his grave in Rhyl municipal cemetery. The white military headstone commemorates **Lieutenant Colonel Arthur Owen Vaughan**, DSO, DCM, OBE, fearless warrior, who persuaded the powers-that-be to establish a Welsh cavalry regiment during the First World War. A

Emrys ap Iwan, Rhewl

taller granite memorial, headed by a Celtic cross, stands in memory of **Owen Rhoscomyl** (1863–1919), who wrote a passionate history of Wales, *Flame-bearers of Welsh History*, in 1905, which was to inspire generations of Welsh schoolchildren with tales of heroism and valour. Though the intensity of his patriotism was rather too strong for some he was, nevertheless, invited by Lloyd George to act as a historical adviser for the pageant during the investiture of Edward as Prince of Wales in Caernarfon in 1911.

ST ASAPH

Inside the cathedral, probably near the Bishop's throne though the exact location is no longer known, lies **William Morgan** (1545–1604), Bishop of St Asaph who, as vicar at Llanrhaeadr-ym-Mochnant, translated the Bible into Welsh, to be published in 1588. Through this remarkable achievement Morgan, more than any other single person, is credited with the preservation of the Welsh language. Certainly the 400th anniversary of this event was considered sufficiently important for the Post Office to issue a set of attractive commemorative postage stamps in 1988.

Outside in the churchyard, near the south wall, lies **William Mathias** (1934–92), professor of music at the University College of North Wales, Bangor, from 1970 to 1988 and regarded as one of the great Welsh musicians of the twentieth century. He came to national prominence in 1981 when he was commissioned by Prince Charles to write a special choral work on the occasion of his wedding to Princess Diana.

Richard Robert Jones (1780–1843), **Dic Aberdaron**, once described as 'one-quarter idiot, three-quarters genius', is buried by a tree near the southern wall of the parish church of St Asaph and St Kentigern, down the hill from the cathedral. He spent his life roaming Wales with his cat, looking and behaving like a tramp, cadging favours as he went. Nevertheless, he is reported to have taught himself as many as thirty-five languages, ancient and modern, though this may be an exaggeration. His one tangible achievement was a Welsh–Greek–Hebrew dictionary compiled in 1831 and 1832, which unfortunately was never published, though a copy can be seen in the National Library of Wales. His gravestone carries two Welsh epitaphs, one of which, in translation reads:

> A linguist eight times greater than all the others
> He was truly a dictionary of every province.
> Death removed his fifteen languages.
> Now, below, he has no languages at all.

TREMEIRCHION

Under the north transept of Corpus Christi church lies **Hester Piozzi** (1741–1821), referred to on her memorial plaque as 'Doctor Johnson's Mrs Thrale'. The wife of Henry Thrale, MP and brewer, she first met Dr Samuel Johnson in 1765, immediately becoming part of his social and literary circle. The Thrales and Dr Johnson went on a tour of north Wales in 1774 and the diary that Mrs Thrale kept of her experiences was far more interesting than Dr Johnson's own account; indeed, he did not find the trip particularly rewarding. As he wrote to a friend:

> Wales has nothing that can much excite or gratify curiosity. The mode of life is entirely English. I am glad I have seen it, though I have seen nothing because I now know there is nothing to be seen.

After Henry Thrale's death in 1781 Hester married an Italian music teacher, Gabriele Piozzi, much to Dr Johnson's dismay.

FLINTSHIRE

CILCAIN

At the top of the village cemetery, on the left-hand side, is a black marble headstone marking the grave of **Gwilym Meredith Edwards** (1917–99). He was one of Wales's most versatile actors, even if many of the characters he played, in films or on television, turned out to be Welsh policemen (*The Blue Lamp*, *Tiger Bay*, *Sexton Blake*, *Z Cars*). A man of strong principles, he was a conscientious objector during the Second World War and a member of the Campaign for Nuclear Disarmament afterwards. He would refuse to accept acting roles which glorified war. He once stood for Parliament as a Plaid Cymru candidate.

HAWARDEN

Herbert John (Viscount) Gladstone (1854–1930), the youngest son of the Liberal Prime Minister, had a respectable political career in his own right. He served as Liberal MP for Leeds from 1880 to 1910 and succeeded Tom Ellis as Liberal Chief Whip in 1899. In this post he negotiated a secret election compact with Ramsay Macdonald, secretary of the Labour Representation Committee, whereby the Liberal and Labour parties agreed not to oppose each other in certain seats in parliamentary elections, a deal which ensured a creditable Labour performance in the 1906 general election. He served as Home Secretary from 1905 to 1910 when, elevated to the peerage, he was appointed the first Governor General of South Africa, a post he held until 1914. His remaining years in domestic politics were mainly spent trying to keep Asquithian Liberalism afloat. He is buried in the family plot in the north-west corner of St Deiniol's churchyard, his substantial tombstone now largely obscured by shrubs.

MOLD

A solid chest-tomb near to the north wall of the parish church marks the grave of **Richard Wilson** (1713/14–82), son of the rector of Penegoes, near Machynlleth, and universally acknowledged as the father of British landscape painting. He is especially remembered for his scenes of Wales, producing particularly striking paintings of Snowdon, Cadair Idris, Cilgerran and Caernarfon castles and of Dinas Brân from Llangollen. One of his best-known works (done, it is said, to clear a debt) was the sign that used to be outside the Loggerheads Inn on the Mold–Ruthin road, though, having disappeared for a time, it now turns out to have been a copy all along. Named 'We three loggerheads' (blockheads) only two heads were depicted, the third being that of the observer.

In the municipal cemetery, just to the right of the car park, is the grave of **Daniel Owen** (1836–95). Born in Mold, where he lived for most of his life, Owen is acknowledged as among the greatest of Welsh novelists, author of such classics as *Rhys Lewis* (1885) and *Enoc Huws* (1891). A bronze statue, the work of Sir William Goscombe John, stands outside the public library and carries Owen's own words: 'Nid i'r doeth a'r deallus yr ysgrifenais, ond i'r dyn cyffredin' (I wrote not for the wise and learned but for the common man).

PICTON

In the rather remote Picton cemetery, up in the hills above Prestatyn, lies **David George Lloyd** (1912–69), a legendary tenor for over three decades, equally at home in the concert halls and opera houses of Europe and on the National Eisteddfod platform. In 1954 he suffered an accident which kept him from the public eye for several years and, although he made a comeback in 1960, his voice was never the same again. In Wales, David Lloyd is probably best remembered for his renderings of popular Welsh songs and hymns, performed on records and on radio programmes such as *Silver Chords*. The names of two of the melodies for ever associated with David Lloyd, 'Hyder' and 'Lausanne', are engraved on the headstone of his grave, on the right-hand side of the cemetery, a few yards from the main path.

TRELAWNYD

Evan Davies (1794–1855), also known by his pseudonym **Eta Delta**, a native of Llanbryn-mair, is believed to have been the first person in Wales to promote total abstinence or teetotalism, establishing in 1835 a teetotal society in the village of Llannerch-y-medd, Anglesey, the first of many set up in Wales. He was a combative character whose extreme views offended many. He argued for instance that bastards, non-teetotallers and those with physical handicaps should have no place in the ministry. He also accused many of his distinguished clerical colleagues of spending too much time developing their egos at the expense of their pastoral duties. He even claimed that much that was written in the 'Blue Books' of 1847 about the ignorance and immorality of the Welsh people was, if unpalatable, probably true. From 1841 until his death he lived in Newmarket (now Trelawnyd). The burial register shows that he was laid to rest in the churchyard of the parish church of St Michael and All Angels on 4 September 1855 but as the churchyard was subject to clearance in the 1960s, with many headstones discarded or relocated, his exact whereabouts are no longer known.

WHITFORD

Thomas Pennant (1726–98) was a gifted writer on natural history, antiquarianism and travel. He is best known for his classic *Tour of Wales* (2 vols, 1778, 1781) which contains the memorable description of Caernarfon castle as 'the most magnificent badge of our subjection'. There is a portrait of Pennant, by Thomas Gainsborough, in the National Museum of Wales. He is buried inside the parish church of St Beuno and St Mary, near the altar. Outside, by the north wall of the churchyard is the chest tomb marking the grave of Pennant's devoted servant, **Moses Griffith** (1747–1819), who accompanied Pennant on his travels and illustrated his books. His tombstone bears the following epitaph, written by Pennant's son:

In memory of Moses Griffith, an ingenious self-taught Artist who accompanied Thomas Pennant, the Historian, in his Tours, whose works he illustrated with his faithful Pencil.

GWYNEDD (CAERNARFONSHIRE)

BANGOR

In the small circular section in the middle of Glanadda cemetery, directly opposite the chapel, lies the Welsh writer and patriot **William Ambrose Bebb** (1894–1955). A founder member of Plaid Genedlaethol Cymru (the Nationalist Party of Wales) he served as the first editor of its newspaper *Y Ddraig Goch* (The Red Dragon), and his writings, including several Welsh textbooks, sought to give their readers a sense of pride in the history and traditions of their small country. He also developed a deep attachment to Brittany, another Celtic nation featured in his books, including his first, *Llydaw* (1929), and it was because of his love of France that, unlike many Plaid Cymru leaders, he strongly supported British entry into the Second World War. His son was the great Welsh wing three-quarter Dewi Bebb (1938–96), one of the few from north Wales to reach the top in rugby union who, after his retirement, pursued a successful career as a television producer. His ashes were scattered at Thornhill crematorium, Cardiff.

Sir Thomas Artemus Jones (1871–1943), the distinguished journalist and lawyer, is buried in the New Cemetery, Llandegai Road. A County Court judge, he did much to encourage the use of Welsh in courts of law, and during the Second World War he was a remarkably humane chairman of the North Wales Conscientious Objectors' Tribunal, upholding 90 per cent of applications for registration as conscientious objectors. Much earlier (in 1908) he had himself been embroiled in legal controversy when he took out a libel action against Hulton Press because the *Sunday Chronicle* had unwittingly used the name Artemus Jones in a defamatory way. The case went to the House of Lords where he won, and thereafter novels have generally carried a disclaimer inserted by prudent publishers along the following lines:

> The characters and events in this book are entirely fictional. No reference to any person, living or dead, is intended, or should be inferred.

He is buried to the right of the main entrance to the cemetery, about fifty yards along section A in the middle row (grave number 77). About fifty yards further on, in the first row (section A, number 50), are the ashes of **Robert Thomas Jenkins** (1881–1969), the distinguished professor of Welsh history at the University College of North Wales, Bangor, and editor of the indispensable work of reference *Y Bywgraffiadur Cymreig hyd 1940* and the English version, *The Dictionary of Welsh Biography down to 1940*. In the section of the cemetery immediately ahead of the main gate, nine rows down, lie the ashes of the celebrated BBC radio producer **Sam Jones** (1898–1974). Based in the Bangor studios as director of programmes he was responsible for such outstanding series as *Awr y Plant*, *Ymryson y Beirdd* and *Wedi'r Oedfa*. By the late 1940s the variety show *Noson Lawen* had become the most popular radio programme in the whole history of Welsh-language broadcasting, attracting a larger Welsh audience than the hugely popular English-language light entertainment programme *ITMA*. He was responsible for bringing the folk-singing talents of the septuagenarian Bob Roberts, Tai'r Felin, to a wide radio audience. The ashes of **Sir Thomas Parry** (1904–85), the eminent scholar and principal of University College of Wales, Aberystwyth, were scattered over the garden of remembrance.

BEDDGELERT

In the churchyard lie the ashes of **Sir Thomas Herbert Parry-Williams** (1887–1975), one of the towering figures of Welsh cultural life in the twentieth century. In 1912 he won both the Chair and the Crown at the same National Eisteddfod, the first time this had been done. He proceeded to repeat the feat in 1915. He held the Chair of Welsh at University College of Wales, Aberystwyth, from 1920 to 1952 and, by the end of his life, his time as a conscientious objector during the First World War far behind him, he had become revered as one of the symbols of the Welsh establishment. He was a dignified pillar of the National Eisteddfod and was rewarded with many honours, including the gold medal of the Honourable Society of Cymmrodorion in 1952 and a knighthood in 1958. Nevertheless, he still enjoyed the respect of such radicals as Carwyn James who used him as a referee for job applications. His celebrated poem 'Hon', reproduced as a poster, adorns the walls of many Welsh homes.

Near to the churchyard, according to legend, lie the remains of Gelert, the faithful hound of Llywelyn the Great. In fact, the sad story was invented by the landlord of the Royal Goat Inn at the end of the eighteenth century to boost the local tourist trade.

BETHESDA

In Coetmor cemetery, above the town, lie two of Wales's most celebrated literary figures of the twentieth century. **Robert Williams Parry** (1884–1956), a kinsman of T. H. Parry-Williams and Thomas Parry, is considered one of the finest British poets of his age, first coming into prominence as the winner of the Chair at the 1910 National Eisteddfod with a poem 'Yr Haf' (The Summer), a literary landmark. Though his overall output was relatively small, gravestones throughout Wales carry sad elegies written by Williams Parry to commemorate young lives sacrificed during battles of the First World War. His grave, now overwhelmed by shrubs, is on the right of the path, not far from the cemetery entrance. At the end of the path, near the workmen's hut, is the grave of **Dafydd Orwig** (1928–96), sometime chairman of Gwynedd County Council and a fierce campaigner in defence of the Welsh language. He once defined diplomacy as 'lying in state'.

Caradog Prichard (1904–80) is buried in the separate, but adjacent, church section of the cemetery. His distinctive slate headstone can be seen to the right of the path leading to the chapel, near to the hedge. Born in the shadow of the Penrhyn slate quarry he, like R. Williams Parry, was an outstanding figure in the history of the National Eisteddfod, winning the Crown in three successive years – 1927 (when he became, at the age of twenty-two, the youngest winner of the event), 1928 and 1929 – and the Chair in 1962. He is, however, best remembered for his only novel, *Un Nos Ola Leuad* (One Moonlit Night), set during the First World War in the district where he spent his formative years. During his journalistic career in London he and his wife Mattie were the centre of a vibrant London Welsh social circle.

CAEATHRO

If Wales's one distinctive contribution to the world of music is the *cymanfa ganu*, the hymn-singing festival, the main credit must go to **John Roberts** (1822–77), **Ieuan Gwyllt**, Calvinistic Methodist minister and author of the still-popular hymn tune 'Moab'. He organized the first *cymanfa ganu* in Aberdare in 1859, and the movement spread like wildfire, using as a primer Roberts's congregational hymn book, *Llyfr Tonau Cynulleidfaol* (1859), regarded by Gareth Williams as the most important book published in Wales during the nineteenth century (*Valleys of Song: Music and Society in Wales 1840–1914*, 1998). It is said that once, while leading a *cymanfa ganu* at Caeathro Calvinistic Methodist chapel, he encountered a revolt from the congregation, who declined to follow his lead. They were upset because the hymn 'Bryn Calfaria', composed by a local musician **William Owen** (1813–93), and still a popular favourite, had been missed out of Roberts's hymn book. The two of them now lie not far from each other in the chapel cemetery. Owen's grave is marked by a handsome brown pedestal and urn near to the main road, and Roberts's by an equally elegant brown marble obelisk, surrounded by railings, about thirty yards further back.

CHWILOG

Eliseus Williams (1867–1926), better known as **Eifion Wyn**, clerk to the North Wales Slate Company, was described by his obituarist in the *Manchester Guardian* as 'Wales's finest lyric poet'. His hymn 'Un fendith dyro im' (Give to me one blessing), sung to Joseph Parry's tune 'Sirioldeb', remains a great favourite at *cymanfâu ganu* to this day, and he is remembered by generations of Sunday school members as the author of the child's prayer:

Dod ar fy mhen dy sanctaidd law,	(Place on my head your sacred hand,
O! dyner Fab y Dyn.	O! Gentle Son of Man.)

His birthplace, 10 Garth Place, Porthmadog, is commemorated by a plaque. A more substantial memorial was erected at his grave in Chwilog cemetery in 1934, being unveiled by none other than David Lloyd George. This can be reached by taking the path straight up from the cemetery gate and proceeding about twenty-five yards along the first turning on the right.

CRICIETH

A few yards from the entrance to the town cemetery stands the Lloyd George family plot dominated by a fine white memorial primarily dedicated to David Lloyd George's daughter **Mair** (1890–1907), her striking bust carved into the marble, the work of Sir William Goscombe John. Others buried within include: David Lloyd George's formidable and long-suffering wife **Dame Margaret Lloyd George** (1866–1941), the first woman JP in Wales; his son **Gwilym, Viscount Tenby** (1894–1967), who, while serving as Home Secretary and Minister for Welsh Affairs (1954–7) announced the choice of Cardiff as capital of Wales; and his daughter **Lady Olwen Carey-Evans** (1892–1990). The most celebrated occupant of the family plot is **Lady Megan Lloyd George** (1902–66), the youngest of David Lloyd George's five children, who, when elected Liberal MP

Goscombe John's bust of Mair Lloyd George

for Anglesey in 1929, became the first woman MP in Wales. A radical throughout her life, it was not surprising that, having lost her seat in 1951, she joined the Labour Party, becoming that party's MP for Carmarthen from 1957 until her death in 1966. Indeed, she took the view that she had not so much deserted the Liberals, rather that the Liberals, by moving to the right, had deserted her. A keen feminist, she turned down her only chance of a government post in the Ministry of Pensions in 1940 because she feared that it would compromise her stance in favour of equal pay and conditions between men and women. She took a leading part in the movement for a Welsh parliament in the 1950s. Though she never married she had a close relationship for twenty years with the peace campaigner Philip Noel-Baker. Understandably, he stayed well clear of her funeral, though Frances Stevenson, Countess Lloyd George, the Prime Minister's second wife, to whom Megan had been implacably hostile, was spotted hovering at the cemetery gate. Immediately behind the plot is the grave of David Lloyd George's brother, **William George** (1865–1967), who practised as a solicitor in Porthmadog almost until his death at the age of 101.

EDERN

One of the most controversial Nonconformist ministers of the twentieth century lies buried in the cemetery at Edern, near Morfa Nefyn. **Thomas Williams** (1895–1958), generally known as **Tom Nefyn**, while a Calvinistic Methodist minister in Tumble, Carmarthenshire, during the 1920s, espoused increasingly unorthodox beliefs, challenging some of the basic tenets of Christianity. This led to his suspension from his denomination in 1928 and the expulsion from Ebenezer chapel of over 200 of his devoted flock, who set up a new meeting house, Llain y Delyn, nearby in the following year. These events brought Tom Nefyn into national prominence for a short while, but by the time the Tumble Christian Fellowship had become fully operational he had returned to his roots in north Wales, where he was accepted back into the fold, leaving many of his erstwhile followers with a deep and lasting sense of betrayal. Nevertheless there were many from Tumble among the 3,000 mourners at the funeral of this much loved pastor nearly thirty years later.

LLANDDEINIOLEN

In the the churchyard, his grave marked by a large stone from his great-grandfather's nearby farm and inscribed 'Athro, Bardd, Llenor' (teacher, poet, man of letters), lies **William John Gruffydd** (1881–1954), one of Wales's greatest literary figures of the twentieth century. The son of a slate quarryman, he was an inspiring professor of Welsh at University College, Cardiff, and served as editor of the influential Welsh literary journal *Y Llenor*, publishing the poetry and prose of all the greatest Welsh writers of the time for nearly thirty years. His own editorial articles were eagerly read for their trenchant views on the issues of the day, though they did not always endear him to his colleagues. Sir Idris Bell once described him as 'something of an *enfant terrible* in Welsh letters, continually in hot water with those whose idea of patriotism is to turn a blind eye to national shortcomings'. He certainly upset a lot of people by opposing (and easily defeating) Saunders Lewis in a by-election for the University of Wales parliamentary seat in 1943, retaining it until its abolition in 1950.

LLANDWROG

John Gwilym Jones (1904–88), university teacher and writer, ranked by many with Saunders Lewis as the greatest twentieth-century playwright in the Welsh language, is buried with his mother and father in the cemetery, having lived in the nearby village of Y Groeslon throughout his life. As far as he was concerned, nothing but a bomb or death itself would have driven him away from there.

LLANDYGÁI

To the right of the path leading to the door of St Tegai's church is a prominent Celtic cross marking the family plot of the Douglas-Pennant dynasty, including **Edward Gordon Douglas-Pennant, 1st Baron Penrhyn** (1800–86), who, although not responsible for building the present Penrhyn Castle, did acquire most of the pictures in the castle's splendid art collection, and entertained Queen Victoria and Prince Albert at Penrhyn in 1859. He was MP for Caernarfon-

shire for twenty years before being elevated to the peerage in 1866. Inside the church, by the altar, is a splendid marble memorial to **Richard Pennant** (1737?–1808), who laid the foundations of the subequent prosperity of the Penrhyn family. The holder of an Irish title, Baron Penrhyn of Penrhyn, Co. Louth, he did a lot for the local community if the handsome tribute on his memorial is anything to go by:

Richard Pennant, Llandygái

He enriched and adorned the demesne and the country around it with buildings, agriculture and plantations, improved the condition of the peasantry, exciting them to habits of industry by employment and laid the foundations of the more important blessing of an advancement in religion and morality by the erection and endowment of St Anne's chapel. His domestic life was distinguished by order, temperance and regularity, an habitual cheerfulness and complacency of temper and a polite and uniform urbanity of manners to persons of every description.

Conspicuously absent from the family plot is George Sholto Douglas-Pennant, 2nd Baron Penrhyn (1836–1907), a fierce opponent of trade unionism, who ran his slate quarries like a feudal lord. His bitter battle with the Bethesda slate quarrymen from 1900 to 1903 was the longest industrial dispute in British history and contributed to the long-term decline of the north Wales slate industry. Perhaps wisely, he was buried at Stoney Stratford, Northamptonshire.

LLANGÏAN

In this Llŷn peninsula churchyard is an ancient stone dating from the fifth or early sixth century with the inscription *Meli Medici Fili Martini Iacit* (Here lies **Melus** the Doctor, son of Martinus), the earliest medical practitioner in Britain whose name we know.

LLANYSTUMDWY

Described by its best-known resident, the writer Jan Morris, as 'now a sort of Lloyd George theme park', Llanystumdwy is where, according to Winston Churchill, 'the greatest Welshman that unconquerable race has produced since the age of the Tudors' is buried. Though born in Manchester, **David Lloyd George** (1863–1945), British Prime Minister from 1916 to 1922, was brought up here in a cobbler's cottage opposite the village pub, and it was here that his view of the world was shaped. He established an early reputation as the radical scourge of the aristocracy, though he was to mellow sufficiently at the end of his life to accept elevation to the House of Lords as Earl Lloyd George of Dwyfor and Viscount Gwynedd. His well-signposted grave by the edge of the river Dwyfor, designed by his friend Sir Clough Williams-Ellis, creator of the Italianate village of Portmeirion, is in a beautiful position.

PENTREFELIN

About half a mile down a narrow lane leading from the main road is the isolated Ynyscynhaearn churchyard, the resting place of **David Owen** (1712?–41), harpist and composer, generally known as **Dafydd y Garreg Wen** (David of the White Rock), after the name of his farmhouse in Ynyscynhaearn. According to tradition, Dafydd y Garreg Wen composed the air of that name on his deathbed, having emerged from a trance during which he had apparently heard the tune in heaven. Its first performance was at his funeral. Nearly 200 years later, on 13 February 1923 the first Welsh words ever broadcast on the BBC were sung by Mostyn Thomas from studio 5WA in Cardiff, to the tune 'Dafydd y Garreg Wen'. The chest tomb, bearing a carving of a harp, is halfway down the church path on the right-hand side, a few yards from the boundary wall.

PISTYLL

The workmanlike acting career of **Rupert Davies** (1916–76), Liverpool-born of Welsh parents, was transformed when he took the part of the pipe-smoking TV detective Maigret. Georges Simenon, who created the character, after meeting Davies, declared: 'At last I have found the perfect Maigret,' and in 1963,

the final year of the series, Rupert Davies was voted TV Actor of the Year. After that, the typecast Davies's acting career went into decline. He is buried in his favourite holiday haunt, and his headstone in St Beuno's churchyard, a little way along the path immediately to the right of the church gate, has the following words, peeping above the long grass:

> Greatly loved by his family and friends. Remembered with affection by thousands who had never met him.

PORTHMADOG
Ronald Stuart Thomas, Anglican priest, controversial Welsh patriot and one of the greatest poets writing in English of the twentieth century, spent his last years in Pentrefelin, and his funeral ('no hymns, no oration, a minimalist formulaic funeral service mainly in Welsh – no doubt all according to RS's wishes', in Ned Thomas's account) was held in the village church. His ashes, however, were interred in St John's churchyard, Porthmadog, where his memorial service was held, the location marked by a small plaque bearing the words 'R. S. Thomas, 1913–2000'.

TREGARTH
Edward Tegla Davies (1880–1967), though he considered himself primarily a Wesleyan Methodist minister, was a popular writer probably best known for two tales, classics of their type, written about, and for, boys: *Hunangofiant Tomi* (Tommy's Autobiography) and *Nedw*. He also wrote one novel, *Gŵr Pen y Bryn* (The Master of Pen y Bryn), set in north Wales during the tithe war of the 1880s. Although he accepted an honorary doctorate from the University of Wales in 1958, he refused the offer of the OBE in 1962, considering such an award inappropriate for a man of his calling. The headstone on his grave, in Tregarth cemetery, simply describes him as 'Minister of the Gospel'.

YNYS ENLLI
Ynys Enlli (Bardsey Island), a remote island off the tip of the Llŷn peninsula, was the location of a monastery in the sixth century and became a popular place of pilgrimage throughout the Middle Ages. Twenty thousand 'saints' are reputed to be buried here in unmarked graves, though the seventeenth-century antiquarian Thomas Fuller, writing in his *Worthies of Wales* (1662), had his doubts:

Where would so many bodies find graves in so petty an island? But I retrench myself, confessing it more facile to find graves in Bardsey for so many saints than saints for so many graves!

Nevertheless, there were enough bones lying around in the nineteenth century for the local farmers to use them for fencing, and they still emerge from the ground from time to time, even now.

GWYNEDD (MERIONETH)

BALA

Buried in Christ Church churchyard, on the left of the path leading to the church door, is **John Puleston Jones** (1862–1925). Though totally blind from the age of eighteen months, he was a brilliant scholar at Balliol College, Oxford (where he was one of the seven founder members of the celebrated Dafydd ap Gwilym Society), and became one of the best respected Calvinistic Methodist ministers of his day, admired by all because of the way he coped with his disability. He travelled everywhere on his own, even by train. 'There is always an angel on every platform,' he used to say. He invented a Braille system for the Welsh language which is still used.

BARMOUTH

One of the most interesting residents of this small town in the late nineteenth century was **Auguste Guyard** (*c.*1809–82), a French social reformer and friend of Lamartine, Victor Hugo and Alexandre Dumas, who had attempted, in vain, to establish a model commune in his home village of Frotey-lez-Vesoul in the teeth of opposition from Church and State. Fleeing France at the time of the Franco-Prussian war he was offered temporary refuge in Barmouth by Mrs G. T. Talbot, a local philanthropist, and was to live at 2 Rock Terrace for the rest of his life, where he was visited by John Ruskin. He had an encyclopedic knowledge of animals and plant life, and when he was not tending his own garden, wearing a long grey coat and a red fez, he would, in broken English, pass on his knowledge to the local people who thought the world of him. After his death he was buried on the hillside behind his house, his headstone bearing the following lines, dictated by the old man to his daughter, the day before his death:

Ci-gît un Semeur qui   (Here lies a sower who, until
Sema jusqu'au tombeau   his death spread the seeds of
Le Vrai, le Bien, le Beau.   Truth, Goodness and Beauty.)

BLAENAU FFESTINIOG

Not far from the entrance to Bethesda cemetery, Manod, is a distinctive slate headstone marking the grave of **David Francis** (1865–1929), universally known as **Y Telynor Dall o Feirion** (the blind harpist of Merioneth), an important influence on the development of harp playing who, during the summer months made a living, at the Belle Vue Hotel, entertaining the hypochondriacs 'taking the cure' at Trefriw Spa. The story goes that on his deathbed, while a harpist was gently playing a tune, he foresaw the moment of his expiry: 'One string is broken on the harp. When the third goes it will be time to say farewell.' And so it came about, enabling the following day's newspapers to print headlines such as 'Drama of blind minstrel' and 'Harp strings snap just before death'. Francis was a very popular man and his funeral was the largest ever witnessed in Blaenau Ffestiniog, with his harp drawn on an open wagon immediately in front of the coffin.

BRYNCRUG
Mary Jones (1784–1864) was the weaver's daughter from Llanfihangel-y-Pennant who was so desperate to acquire a bible that, at the age of sixteen, having saved up her pennies, she walked to Bala, a hard journey of some twenty-five miles, to buy one from the Reverend Thomas Charles. Not having one to sell, and impressed by Mary's piety, he gave her his own copy, and this incident inspired Charles to establish the British and Foreign Bible Society in order to ensure a ready supply of bibles for all who wanted one. The rest of Mary's life was worthy if unspectacular. She married a local weaver, settled in Bryncrug, near Tywyn, and took up beekeeping to supplement their meagre income. Her bible is now

preserved in Cambridge University Library. Her grave may be found by taking the path round the back of Bethel chapel and bearing left towards the cemetery wall.

CAPEL CELYN

Sadly Capel Celyn no longer exists except during periods of exceptional drought. Then, Llyn Celyn, the reservoir created there by Liverpool Corporation in the early 1960s in defiance of Welsh public opinion, dries up sufficiently to reveal the remains of a once vibrant community. On the A4212 at the northern shore of the lake stands a building bearing the following notice:

> This building together with the Garden of Remembrance was erected as a Memorial for the Chapel and the Burial Ground of Capel Celyn now submerged by Llyn Celyn.

In the small garden of remembrance are gathered the headstones from the original graveyard.

CEFNDDWYSARN

Under a Celtic cross, standing prominently in the centre of the Calvinistic Methodist chapel cemetery, lies **Thomas Edward Ellis** (1859–99), the most prominent spokesman for the cause of Wales in the late nineteenth century and regarded by many as the 'Parnell of Wales'. He was Liberal MP for his native Merioneth from 1886 until his death and for some years was a passionate advocate of Welsh Home Rule, but it was widely believed that government office during the 1890s, and his appointment as Liberal Chief Whip in 1894, diverted his priorities elsewhere. Nevertheless, his untimely death was greatly mourned and his statue stands proudly in Bala High Street. A few yards away from his grave, nearer the chapel, lies Ellis's good friend **David Robert Daniel** (1859–1931), temperance and trade-union organizer and close confidant of all the leading Welsh Liberals of his time, including David Lloyd George, with whom he fell out over British policy during the First World War. Again, not far from Tom Ellis lies one of 'The Three Bobs' (Y Tri Bob), **Robert Lloyd** (1888–1961), a lifelong zealot for all things Welsh (he had been baptized by that supreme Welsh patriot Michael D. Jones). Universally known by his bardic name **Llwyd o'r Bryn**, he was a major force in the eisteddfod movement and after his death the annual Llwyd o'r Bryn prize for recitation was established by the National Eisteddfod in his memory.

DOLGELLAU

A couple of miles east of Dolgellau, at Tabor, just off the A470, is the evocative Tyddyn Garreg Quaker cemetery, established in the seventeenth century by Owen Lewis, a pioneer of the cause and, according to one account, 'subjected to extortionate fines and violent persecution' for his faith. Among those buried in the cemetery is **Dorothy Owen** of Upper Dewisbren (*c.*1751–93), known in Welsh as Dorti, an indefatigable champion for the movement who, according to T. Mardy Rees in his book *The Quakers in Wales* (1925):

> began to bear public testimony unto the Truth at the age of twenty-three. She travelled on foot over the Welsh mountains to meetings, and walked to the Yearly Meeting in London and back . . . Dorothy Owen lived a consecrated life, and turned many to righteousness.

HARLECH

In St Tanwg's churchyard, under a Celtic cross, lie the parents of the poet Robert Graves. His father, **Alfred Perceval Graves** (1846–1931), was no mean literary figure himself, author of many songs including 'Father O'Flynn', and the compiler of a popular anthology of *Welsh Poetry Old and New* (1912). He was also a founder member of the Welsh Folk Song Society. In recognition of his contribution to Welsh cultural life he was admitted to the Gorsedd of Bards at the National Eisteddfod in Blaenau Ffestiniog in 1898.

LLANBEDR

Just to the right of the churchyard gate is a striking memorial, in the form of a slender slate pyramid, to one of the most prominent, if least popular, figures in the British motor industry for over thirty years, **Sir John Black** (1895–1965). During the 1920s and 1930s he successfully managed first the Hillman, then the Standard car companies and during the war he made a major contribution to the production of aero-engines, for which he received a knighthood. A vain man, likened by many to Mussolini, he had an oppressive, even tyrannical management style. He expected his managers to stand when he entered the room and resented the fact that trade union representatives would not do likewise. In 1953 he became chairman of the Standard Car Company but his erratic behaviour proved too much for his colleagues and after a few months he was forced to retire, having sacked some of his top managers during the firm's Christmas party.

LLANFAIR

Whether or not people know her name, **Siân Owen** (1837–1927) is one of the most famous of Welsh icons, being the lady with the Devil's face in her shawl in Sydney Curnow Vosper's celebrated painting *Salem*. Though she died at the ripe old age of ninety, the rather uncomfortable epitaph on her gravestone, in St Mary's churchyard, may reflect a far from easy life – she was a widow for thirty-four years and two of her grandsons were killed in the First World War; she may also have been disturbed by the controversial aspects of the picture in which she was the central figure:

Cystuddiwyd fi yn ddirfawr: bywha fi, O Arglwydd yn ôl dy air.

(I am afflicted above measure: give me life, O Lord, according to Thy word.)

Psalms 119:107

The name on her headstone, a few yards to the left of the church door, is shown as Jane Owens. Buried five rows eastwards from her grave is **Thomas Iorwerth Ellis** (1899–1970), the posthumous son of T. E. Ellis, the Liberal politician. He served from 1941 to 1967 as the secretary of Undeb Cymru Fydd (The New Welsh Nation), an influential pressure group dedicated to the language and culture of Wales. He was also a popular author, perhaps best known for the biography of his father and as a contributor to the 'Crwydro' series of travel books. In his book *Crwydro Meirionnydd* (1954) he referred several times to **Ellis Wynne** (1671–1734), rector of Llanfair church for many years and the author, in 1703, of what is regarded as one of the classics of Welsh literature, *Gweledigaetheu y Bardd Cwsc* (The Visions of the Sleeping Bard). Wynne is buried inside Llanfair church, under the altar.

LLAN FFESTINIOG

Travellers along the B4391 between Maentwrog and Llan Ffestiniog will notice on top of a hill on their right-hand side a railed enclosure, now becoming increasingly overwhelmed by shrubs and bushes. Within the enclosure is the grave of **William Charles Wynn**, **4th Baron Newborough** (1873–1916), a lieutenant in the Welsh Guards during the First World War. At the time of his death in 1916 the *Western Mail* reported that he had succumbed to wounds received in France though it seems that he actually died of a chill caught in the trenches. Be that as it may, he had left instructions in his will that he should be buried on his estate 'in the simplest manner compatible with decency on the summit of the bluff, from which spot is my favourite view of the Vale of Festiniog'.

LLANFOR

Lloyd Price family vault, Llanfor

Richard John Lloyd Price (1843–1923), the squire of Rhiwlas, near Bala, was a colourful member of one of the leading landowning families in north Wales. He was a distiller of what he considered fine whiskey, his distillery at Frongoch (by then closed) being used as an internment camp for German prisoners and Irish republicans (including Michael Collins) during the First World War. He was a keen sportsman who is credited as the inventor of the modern sheepdog trials, the first one taking place on his land in October 1873. The barn-like family vault at the top end of Llanfor churchyard, where he lies, carries the following inscription:

> As to my latter end I go
> To meet my Jubilee,
> I bless the good horse Bendigo
> Who built this tomb for me.

In some books Lloyd Price is credited as being the owner of Bendigo, a racehorse that won the Derby. In fact he never owned the horse, nor did it ever win the Derby. Nevertheless, Bendigo was one of the great racehorses of the late nineteenth century, winning a string of races in the mid-1880s, including the Eclipse Stakes, the Lincoln Handicap and the Cambridgeshire, feats which would undoubtedly have made good money for the punters, including, so it would seem, R. J. Lloyd Price.

LLANFROTHEN

A prominent memorial stone in the centre of the new cemetery, Llanfrothen, about three rows from the entrance, marks the grave of **Robert Owen** (1885–1962), universally known as **Bob Owen, Croesor**. He was one of 'The Three Bobs' ('Y Tri Bob') of Merioneth, immortalized by Robin Williams in his celebrated recorded lecture (1965) and later the book *Y Tri Bob* (1971); the other two were Bob Lloyd, Llwyd o'r Bryn, and Bob Roberts, Tai'r Felin. Bob Owen, a clerk at the local quarry, was a prodigious collector of books and rare manuscripts and, despite his limited resources, he is said to have amassed nearly 50,000 items in his day, crammed into his little house. He had an encyclopedic knowledge of Welsh people and places and, though lacking any formal qualifications, was acknowledged as an authority on the history of the Welsh in America. In 1931 he was awarded an honorary degree of MA from the University of Wales for his contribution to Welsh scholarship, attracting some patronizing comments from the English press at the time. Some years later he was granted an OBE, an accolade which rather pleased him, if not some of his Welsh nationalist friends.

Behind St Brothen's Church, **Robert Roberts** now lies peacefully enough, though the circumstances of his burial in 1888 were highly controversial at the time. In contravention of the Burial Act of 1880 the local rector had, using a legal technicality, refused to allow Roberts, a strong Nonconformist, to be buried next to his daughter. The local people thereupon broke open the church gate and buried him just the same. The Llanfrothen Church Case went to court, where the Roberts family, advised by the eloquent young solicitor David Lloyd George, were finally vindicated, symbolizing a victory by the Welsh people over an insensitive and alien Church. The church made the news again in 1979 when the parishioners objected to the installation therein of a memorial to their most celebrated, though admittedly agnostic, local resident **Sir Clough Williams-Ellis** (1883–1978). The memorial, made by his friend Jonah Jones, can be seen at Portmeirion, and his ashes were mainly scattered in the gardens of his home in Llanfrothen, Plas Brondanw.

LLANUWCHLLYN

At the entrance to the village are bronze statues, created by the sculptor Jonah Jones, of two of Wales's greatest patriots. **Sir Owen Morgan Edwards** (1858–1920), scholar and educationalist, who, as a

pupil at the village school, had proudly worn the Welsh Not round his neck as a badge of honour, was determined to instil in the ordinary people of Wales a sense of pride in their history, language and culture, through such books as *Wales* (1901) in the Stories of the Nations series and such influential periodicals as *Cymru* and *Cymru'r Plant.* In 1907 he became the first Chief Inspector of Schools in Wales, from which position he sought to transform the standing of Welsh in schools. In presenting Sir Owen Edwards (he was knighted in 1916) to the University of Wales for an

Sir Owen Morgan Edwards, Llanuwchllyn

honorary doctorate Sir John Morris-Jones proclaimed: 'There is no one alive today who has done so much to prolong the life of the Welsh language.' His grave is located in Pandy cemetery, in the centre of the village, entered through an elegant gateway erected to his memory.

His son, **Sir Ifan ab Owen Edwards** (1895–1970), is buried in the cemetery on the outskirts of the village, on the left-hand side, about halfway down. The striking modernist memorial over his grave was designed by his son Prys. Sir Ifan launched in 1922 what became his life's work, the youth movement Urdd Gobaith Cymru (The Welsh League of Youth), the aim of which was to:

> create an undefiled Welsh Wales, not for its own sake, not in any attempt to make Wales superior to other countries, but in order that Wales can play its part in bringing peace to a world which today is too ready to display a spirit of antagonism and war.

At the height of its influence in the mid–1930s the Urdd could boast a membership of 50,000. Ifan was a pioneer in other respects too. In 1935 he produced *Y Chwarelwr* (The Quarryman), the first talking picture ever made in the Welsh language. In 1939, partly in order to create a totally Welsh-speaking environment in which his young son could be educated, he established, in Aberystwyth, the first primary school in Wales where pupils were taught through the medium of Welsh. He was knighted for his services to Wales in 1947.

A mile or two outside the village, in the small cemetery adjoining the historic, but now closed Hen Gapel, are buried, side by side, **Michael Jones** (1787–1853) and his son **Michael Daniel Jones** (1822–98), who succeeded him as the principal of Bala Independent College, responsible for the training of Independent ministers. Both father and son were strong personalities, frequently feuding with their co-religionists over matters of doctrine and organization, but when it came to controversy Michael D. Jones was truly in a league of his own. He detested all things English and vigorously denounced every sign of servility amongst his compatriots, leading him to champion the establishment of a brand new colony in the Chubut valley in Patagonia, miles from anywhere, Nonconformist in religion and Welsh in language. In 1865, the *Mimosa* left Liverpool carrying 153 would-be settlers and, although the early years were hard, they eventually succeeded in creating a colony which was to retain its essential Welshness up to the Second World War. Michael D. Jones did not go to Patagonia himself though he sank, and lost, a lot of his own money in the project. His son, Llwyd ap Iwan, who did go out, was murdered in 1909 by surviving members of Butch Cassidy and the Sundance Kid's gang.

LLANYCIL

A mile or so south of Bala, near the lake, is St Beuno's churchyard where the **Reverend Thomas Charles** (1755–1814) is buried, just by the east wall of the church. He is credited with pioneering, from about 1789, the Sunday school movement in Wales, which did so much to inculcate the democratic spirit in her people during the nineteenth century. The Sunday schools needed bibles, which resulted in Thomas Charles and others founding the British and Foreign Bible Society in 1804. Four years earlier the problem had been drawn forcibly to his attention by Mary Jones who had walked a journey of twenty-five miles to buy one from him and, not having one to sell, he gave her his own. Next to his grave is that of **Lewis Edwards** (1809–87), husband of Charles's granddaughter and for fifty years principal of Bala Calvinistic Methodist College. He was a major force in the intellectual life of Wales in the nineteenth century and, as a supporter of the establishment of English-language chapels in Wales, he crossed swords with Emrys ap Iwan, the fervent nationalist. **Bob Roberts, Tai'r Felin** (1870–1951), the legendary singer of Welsh folk-

songs, star of the Welsh variety show *Noson Lawen* when he was well into his seventies, and the third of 'The Three Bobs' ('Y Tri Bob'), is also buried in the churchyard. The grave can be found by taking the grass path to the left of the main entrance and after proceeding for about fifty yards looking a few feet to the right.

LLANYMAWDDWY

The distinguished physician **Sir William Roberts** (1830–99) is buried in the churchyard. From 1873 to 1889 he was professor of medicine at Owen's College, later to become the University of Manchester, and was a pioneer in the science leading to the discovery of pennicillin, fifty years before Sir Alexander Fleming got the credit for it.

MALLWYD

Inside the splendid church of St Tydecho, to the south of the chancel, is the resting place of **Dr John Davies** (*c.*1567–1644), rector of the parish for forty years and described on his gravestone as 'A great Welsh scholar'. He was responsible for much of the work on the revised Welsh translation of the Bible in 1620 and also published a Welsh–Latin dictionary (1632) and a Welsh grammar, *Antiquae Linguae Britannicae . . . Rudimenta* (1621), which contains this resounding declaration, quoted by Meic Stephens in his book *The Literary Pilgrim in Wales*:

> It is impossible to believe that God would have seen fit to keep this language until these days, after so many crises in the history of the nation . . . had He not intended His name to be called and His great work to be proclaimed in it.

On the north wall of the church there is a marble tablet in his memory, written in Latin.

TALSARNAU

In the isolated churchyard at Llanfihangel-y-traethau, near Talsarnau, where he was a churchwarden for many years, lies the writer **Richard Hughes** (1900–76), best known as the author of *A High Wind in Jamaica* (1929) and *A Fox in the Attic* (1961). His play *Danger* (1924) was the first play ever broadcast on the radio. His grave is on the north side of the churchyard near to a large yew tree. To the left of the churchyard gate lies **William David Ormsby Gore, 5th Earl of Harlech** (1918–85), who was British Ambassador to the United States of America during the presidency of J. F. Kennedy. Also buried in the churchyard is that eighteenth-century oddity, **Mari Evans 'Y Fantell Wen'** (of the white robe) (1735–89) who, claiming to be 'betrothed of Christ', once went through a spectacular 'marriage' ceremony in Ffestiniog church, and gathered around her a substantial crowd of followers, all dressed in white robes. She proclaimed herself immortal so, when she died at Talsarnau, she was for some time left unburied to await the Second Coming, until the local parish constable intervened in the interests of public health.

TYWYN
Inside St Cadfan's Church, opposite the door, is a gravestone carrying the earliest surviving inscription in the Welsh language, dating from between the seventh and ninth centuries. Though damaged through use as a gatepost until the eighteenth century, the stone is said to have marked the grave of Cingen or Cun, wife of Celyn, depending on whether one follows Sir John Morris-Jones's or Sir Ifor Williams's reading of the inscription.

MERTHYR TYDFIL

ABERFAN
In the cemetery above the village, in two long rows, lie the innocent victims of negligent industrialization, when, on 21 October 1966, a coal tip engulfed the local primary school and surrounding buildings, killing 116 children and 28 adults. A whole generation was lost in an instant and scarcely anyone in this close-knit community was untouched by the tragedy. The gravestones carry poignant messages like this:

> The parting was so sudden,
> One day we will know why,
> But the saddest part of all,
> We never said goodbye.

Aberfan

Many gravestones record that, with the passing of the years, grieving parents have been reunited with their children.

CEFNCOEDYCYMER

In the cemetery lies **Sir William Thomas Lewis** (1837–1914), the greatest industrial magnate in south Wales at the beginning of the twentieth century and referred to by Sidney and Beatrice Webb as 'the best-hated man in the Principality', an implacable opponent of organized trade unionism. He was mainly responsible for the development of Cardiff docks, had major interests in the south Wales coalfields and owned the Universal Steam Coal Company at Senghennydd, the scene of the worst mining disaster in British history in 1913, when 439 miners lost their lives following an underground explosion. His involvement on various royal commissions earned him a knighthood in 1885 (upgraded to a baronetcy in 1896) and in 1911 he joined the peerage as Baron Merthyr of Senghennydd. The family vault, topped by a large Celtic cross, can be reached by taking the path left from the car park, turning sharp right where the path forks. If W. T. Lewis was Lord Merthyr, **Eddie Thomas** (1925–97) was undoubtedly 'Mr Merthyr'. After a boxing career during which he won the Welsh, British, European and Empire heavyweight boxing crowns, he became an outstanding boxing manager and promoter, as well as being a susccessful businessman and mayor of Merthyr. However, his ashes lie anonymously in the grave of his parents, at the far northern end

72

of the cemetery (plot number F 8/12). In the extension to Cefncoed cemetery which runs alongside the A470 Merthyr bypass, on the left, near to the entrance, lies Eddie Thomas's greatest protégé, **Howard Winstone** (1939–2000). Winner of the bantamweight gold medal at the Empire Games in Cardiff in 1958 he had an outstanding professional boxing career, winning the British featherweight championship in 1961 and the European crown two years later. In 1968 he briefly held the World featherweight championship and was awarded the MBE. Despite a series of business failures he retained the affection and respect of his home town throughout his life, becoming a freeman of the borough, and on the day of his funeral the town was brought to a standstill.

Jewish cemetery, Cefncoedycymer

Opposite Cefncoed cemetery, on the other side of the A470, is the small and easily missed Jewish cemetery where generations of members of the Jewish communities of the south Wales valleys are buried, their headstones inscribed in English and Hebrew. This evocative place has been eloquently commemorated by the journalist Grahame Davies in the poem 'Merthyr Jewish Cemetery', which, originally written in Welsh, is included in the poet's anthology *The Chosen People – Wales and the Jews* (2002).

In the cemetery to the left of Hen Dŷ Cwrdd Unitarian chapel lie the remains of **Lucy Thomas** (1781–1847). Following her husband's death she carried on the family coalmining business in Merthyr and the Cynon valley. Though unable to write, signing her name with a cross, she was a shrewd operator, as John Nixon, another coalowner, once observed:

She sat in her office, a wooden hut near the pit's mouth, and traded for cash, placing in a basket over her head the monies which she received for her coal.

By the 1840s, she had become the fifth largest coal-shipper out of Cardiff, being universally known as 'Mother of the Welsh steam-coal trade'. She died of typhoid fever at the age of sixty-six, having outlived three of her four sons. Near to St Tydfil's church in Merthyr Tydfil stands an elaborate fountain commemorating Lucy and her husband Robert, erected by Sir W. T. Lewis, Lord Merthyr, who married Lucy's granddaughter.

DOWLAIS TOP

The now sadly derelict and inaccessible St John's church is the resting place of **Sir Josiah John Guest** (1785–1852), the owner of the Dowlais Iron Company, the largest and most advanced ironworks in the world in the early nineteenth century. He was also the Liberal MP for Merthyr Tydfil from 1832 to the time of his death, having previously represented Honiton as a Canningite Tory between 1826 and 1830. When he acquired a country estate at Canford, Dorset, in the 1840s he achieved one of his main ambitions by becoming a member of the landed gentry. Nevertheless, his funeral in Merthyr was reported to have been witnessed by 20,000 mourners. His celebrated wife Lady Charlotte Guest (1812–95), the translator of the *Mabinogion*, went on to marry her son's tutor, eventually settled in Canford and was buried in the churchyard there.

PANT

Johnny Owen (1956–80), dubbed 'Bionic' and the 'Matchstick Man' by south Wales boxing fans, had won twenty-five out of his twenty-seven professional fights, including the Welsh, British and European bantamweight titles, before that fateful day in September 1980 when he fought Lupe Pintor for the World championship in Los Angeles. After a gruelling contest Owen was floored in the final round and was to lie in a coma for six weeks until his death. His funeral witnessed the greatest outpouring of grief in the south Wales valleys since the Aberfan disaster, and Muhammad Ali himself sent a wreath. An appeal fund raised £123,250 in the space of a few weeks, some of which paid the cost of the headstone on his grave (number MJ 10) in Pant cemetery about 100 yards immediately to the right of the main entrance, by the cemetery wall. At the brow of the hill, by the path leading left from the main entrance, is the grave of **John**

Collins (1877–1951), whose funeral was affected by an overtime ban by the local gravediggers. He had been awarded the Victoria Cross 'for conspicuous bravery, resource and leadership' during action in Palestine in 1917, a year later obtaining the DCM. After the war, he worked as a miner, a labourer and a security guard in the Merthyr area. There is a nice modern memorial to Merthyr's only VC in the grounds of St Tydfil's parish church.

TROEDYRHIW

Anthony Hill (1784–1862) was the head of the Plymouth ironworks which, in the 1830s, had the largest blast furnace in the world. A local magistrate, he played a leading role on the side of law and order during the Merthyr riots in 1831 and, as a monoglot English-speaker, he must certainly have felt uncomfortable in the midst of the local population, the vast majority of whom spoke Welsh as their mother tongue. He once observed, with some regret, that:

> the Welsh people will not be driven and they are strongly attached to their language. The efforts being made to promote the greater spread of the native Welsh language are a great bar to the improvement of the people.

In 1852 he built a parish church in Troedyrhiw, stipulating that only he should ever be buried there. Following his death ten years later, no fewer than three coffins were placed in the specially prepared vault under the altar. The inner, elm coffin, lined with Welsh flannel, contained his body; this was placed in a lead casket which, in turn, was enclosed in an outer oak coffin.

VAYNOR

The youngest son of William Crawshay II (the 'Iron King'), **Robert Thompson Crawshay** (1817–79) was given the family home, Cyfarthfa Castle, and Cyfarthfa ironworks by his father, and he ran the business until the 1870s when it closed temporarily. He was a pioneer photographer, and in 1838 he established the Cyfarthfa Band which, during the mid-nineteenth century, was recognized as one of the leading brass bands in the country. Despite this and other contributions to the life of the local community, Crawshay was not a popular man; nor was he an easy father. For whatever reason, he chose the epitaph on his tomb himself:

God forgive me.

This appears on a ten-ton slab of concrete which some said was intended to prevent his ghost from rising up at the time of the Resurrection. The grave, surrounded by sturdy iron railings, lies straight ahead from the entrance to Vaynor churchyard.

MONMOUTHSHIRE

ABERGAVENNY

St Mary's Priory church, one of the largest parish churches in Wales, houses one of the finest collections of tombs and sculptures in Britain, all recently restored at great expense. The best monuments are located in the Herbert Chapel, including the tombs of **Sir William ap Thomas** (d.1446) and his wife, of their son **Sir Richard Herbert** (beheaded after the battle of Banbury in 1469) and of **Sir Richard Herbert of Ewyas** (d.1510). Thomas Churchyard's book *The Worthines of Wales* (1587) contains an eloquent poem describing the fine tombs in the church, including that of **David Lewis** (1520?–84), who, in 1571, became the first principal of Jesus College, Oxford, that Mecca for generations of aspiring Welsh students:

> A friend of myne who lately dyed,
> That Doctor Lewis hight,
> Within that Church his Tombe I spyed,
> Well wrought and fayre to sight.
> O Lord (quoth I) we all must dye,
> No lawe, nor learnings lore,
> No judgement deepe, nor knowledge hye,
> No riches lesse or more,
> No office, place, nor calling great,
> No worldly pompe at all,
> Can keepe us from the mortall threat
> Of death, when God doth call.

CHEPSTOW

Henry Marten (1602–80), according to John Aubrey 'a great lover of pretty girls', and MP for Berkshire, was one of the most hardline anti-royalists during the Civil War and was a leading advocate of Charles I's trial and execution. After signing the King's death warrant, he and Oliver Cromwell proceeded to flick ink into each other's faces with their pens, like schoolchildren. He made no attempt to flee abroad at the restoration of the monarchy and was imprisoned first in the Tower, then at Windsor castle, whence he was removed as 'an eyesore to his Majesty', and finally at Chepstow castle. There he lived with his wife and servants in some comfort for so many years that a tower is now named after him. After his death, Marten was buried in St Mary's church, first in the chancel but later near to the main door, where his now worn gravestone carries this epitaph, written by Marten himself:

> Here or elsewhere, all's one to you or me,
> Earth, air or water gripes my ghostless dust,
> None knows how soon to be by fire set free,
> Reader, if you an oft tried rule will trust.
> You'll gladly do and suffer what you must.
> My life was spent with serving you and you,
> And death's my pay, it seems, and welcome too,
> Revenge destroying but itself, while I
> To birds of prey leave my old cage and fly,
> Examples preach to the eye; care then (mine says)
> Not how you send but how you spend your days.

LLANFOIST

At the top end of the parish churchyard, stands an imposing obelisk marking the grave of one of south Wales's great nineteenth-century industrial entrepreneurs, **Crawshay Bailey** (1789–1872), owner of ironworks and coal mines and a railway pioneer in the Cynon valley. His exploits so fired the popular imagination that he was immortalized in an interminable song which remains popular to this day with rugby teams returning home after the game:

Crawshay Bailey, Llanfoist

> Cosher Bailey had an engine,
> She was puffin' and a-blowing,
> And she had such mighty power
> She could go a mile an hour.

And so on for over forty more verses.

Llanfoist church lies at the foot of the Blorenge mountain. At its summit is the grave of **Foxhunter**, the celebrated showjumper which carried **Harry Llewellyn** (1911–99) to a gold medal at the Helsinki Olympic Games of 1952. After Sir Harry's death (knighted in 1977, he inherited his father's baronetcy the following year) his ashes were scattered by the horse's grave.

Not far from the parish church is Llanfoist cemetery, where lie the ashes of the writer **Alexander Cordell** (1914–97), whose real name was **George Alexander Graber**. He made his reputation as the chronicler of life in industrial south Wales, depicting such dramatic episodes as the Merthyr Rising, the Rebecca riots and Chartism. His best-known book was *Rape of the Fair Country* (1959). Despite his popularity he was generally regarded as rather a phoney in Welsh literary circles; Harri Webb called him 'Alexander Cor-blimey'. Found at a lonely spot near the top of the Horseshoe Pass in Denbighshire, his body surrounded by family photographs, pills and half a bottle of brandy, he was first assumed to have committed suicide, depressed after the death of his second wife, but the inquest concluded that he had, in fact, died of a heart attack. His elegant resting place, a little to the north-west of the chapel, in the middle of the cemetery, contains both his ashes and those of his first wife **Rosina**, 'the first, the loveliest and the best and then along came Donnie, her friend . . . to both wives I owe so much'.

LLANGATTOCK-VIBON-AWEL

Charles Stewart Rolls (1877–1910), third son of the 1st Baron Llangattock, was a motor-car enthusiast who was arrested in 1895 for driving his new Peugeot from London to Cambridge faster than the regulation speed of four miles an hour and without employing a man with a red flag to walk in front. Even so the journey took him nearly twelve hours. Ten years later, he and F. H. Royce formed the legendary car company with him as technical managing director and Royce as chief engineer. In 1910, Rolls became the first person to fly across the English Channel and back without stopping.

Unfortunately, a month later he was killed in a flying tournament at Bournemouth, thereby becoming the first Briton to die in an aviation accident. He was buried next to his father under an elegant Celtic cross in the south-east corner of the churchyard.

LLANOVER

The elaborate chest-tomb of **Sir Benjamin Hall**, Baron Llanover of Llanover and Abercarn (1802–67), and his wife **Augusta, Lady Llanover** (1802–96) dominates the churchyard of St Bartholomew's church. Member of Parliament for Monmouth, Sir Benjamin became Commissioner for Works in 1855, and the great bell in the clock tower at Westminster, 'Big Ben', installed during his period of office, was called after him. He was elevated to the peerage in 1859. He, and particularly his wife, were vigorous champions of all things Welsh. She was an enthusiastic patron of Welsh cultural and literary events and people. She invented the 'traditional' Welsh costume and ran her household on what she considered to be authentic Welsh lines. Since the countryside around Llanover was almost entirely anglicized she imported a number of Welsh-speaking Methodists from Cardiganshire into the neighbourhood, together with their pastor, wearing a regulation beard. At her funeral, she was escorted to her grave by twenty maidens dressed in their Welsh costumes.

MONMOUTH

In St Mary's churchyard, near to the east wall of the church, is a most unusual headstone commemorating **John Renie** (1799?–1832), a local painter and decorator who was, according to his obituary in the local newspaper, 'a man of extraordinary natural abilities and was impressed with the highest and most romantic enthusiasm for rational liberty'. Indeed, his early death was attributed to over-exertion in support of the Reform candidate at the 1832 general election. His headstone is a mass of random letters concealing his name so that, by the time the Devil had worked out who he was, Renie's soul would already have arrived in heaven, safe and sound.

USK

In the churchyard of the Priory church, near to the west door, is the grave of **Saint David Lewis** (1617–79), the last Welsh Catholic martyr. A highly regarded local Jesuit priest, active in the border country and widely known as 'tad y tlodion' (father of the poor), he was falsely accused of treason during the anti-Catholic hysteria at the time of the 'Popish plot' and eventually executed in Usk in

August 1679. His gravestone is now worn smooth and next to it a new stone has been laid, recording the fact that Lewis, beatified in 1929, was one of forty English and Welsh martyrs canonized by Pope Paul VI in October 1970. About thirty yards from the north door of the church is a large flat tombstone which marks the grave of **Philip Mason** who died in 1772 aged fifty-one, weighing over thirty-four stones. In the north-west corner of the churchyard is the rather more elegant resting place of **Sir Matthew Digby Wyatt** (1820–77), the well-known architect, his polished granite tomb having been designed by his even better-known architect brother, T. H. Wyatt.

Inside the church, under the floor near the organ, lie the remains of **Adam of Usk** (1352?–1430), a lawyer at the centre of some of the momentous events of the reigns of Richard II and Henry IV, recording them in his Chronicle which became one of the chief sources for the history of those times. On the south-east side of the screen is a brass strip, dating from the time of his death, containing the oldest epitaph in the Welsh language still extant. An English translation, available in the church, reads as follows:

> The most skilled advocate of London
> and *judge of the world* by gracious privilege –
> may the heavenly abode be thine, good sir!
> After fame, to the tomb, from the bench,
> lo! a Solomon of wisdom,
> Adam Usk is sleeping here,
> the clever doctor of ten commotes –
> behold a place full of learning!

NEATH and PORT TALBOT

ABERAVON

In the centre of St Mary's churchyard, in the shadow of the M4 motorway, lies **Richard Lewis**, known to all as **Dic Penderyn**

(1808/9–31), his grave marked by a small Celtic cross. A labourer, he was arrested as one of the ringleaders of the Merthyr Rising of 1831 and, although there was no credible evidence against him, he was found guilty as an example to others. Despite a petition signed by 11,000 people and the tireless efforts of the Quaker ironmaster Joseph Tregelles Price, Dic Penderyn was publicly hanged in Cardiff on 13 August 1831, uttering, in Welsh, the cry 'O Lord, this is injustice'. His body, accompanied by huge crowds, was taken to his birthplace for burial, and his grave is still a place of pilgrimage for those wishing to honour Wales's first working-class martyr.

ABERDULAIS
Dowlais-born **Robert Rees** (1841–92), **Eos Morlais**, was Wales's most celebrated tenor during the late nineteenth century and it was he who sang 'Hen Wlad fy Nhadau' at the Royal Albert Hall in 1887, in the presence of the Prince of Wales, who was attending the National Eisteddfod for the first time. Equally at home performing grand opera, Victorian ballads and traditional Welsh airs, it is said that he sang 'Y Deryn Pur' on his deathbed. He is buried in the centre of the Calvinistic Methodist chapel cemetery, up a steep hill from the main road, about thirty yards from the chapel door.

CADOXTON-JUXTA-NEATH
By the main path through St Catwg's churchyard, to the right of the church door, stands a splendid 'murder stone' bearing the following inscription:

> 1823. To record Murder. This stone was erected over the body of Margaret Williams, aged 26, a native of Carmarthenshire living in service in this parish, who was found dead with marks of violence upon her person in a ditch on the marsh below this churchyard on the morning of Sunday, 14th July, 1822.
>
> Although the savage murderer escapes for a season the detection of man, yet God hath set His mark upon him, either for time or eternity. And the cry of blood will assuredly pursue him to a certain and terrible but rightful judgment.
>
> Canys nyni a adwaenom y neb a ddywedodd myfi biau dial, myfi a dalaf, medd yr Arglwydd.
>
> (For we know who said: vengeance is mine, I will recompense, saith the Lord).

81

The headstone was erected so as to face a row of cottages on the hillside where the suspected murderer was believed to live, and it is said that not long afterwards one of the residents sailed from Swansea on a cargo boat to start a new life overseas.

MARGAM

Probably the most influential landowner in Glamorgan in the nineteenth century, **Christopher Rice Mansel Talbot** (1803–90) was certainly Britain's wealthiest commoner (he had no title though he was an FRS) and was responsible for the industrial development of Port Talbot, the town that bears his name. He and his family looked down on their town from a magnificent Gothic edifice at Margam, built in the 1830s and which is now maintained by the local council. Talbot was the local MP from 1830 until his death, a distinctly moderate Liberal who, nevertheless, managed to fend off all attempts by the more radical members of his constituency party to replace him, and in 1874 he acquired the status of 'Father of the House of Commons'. Talbot and his family rest in a side chapel to the left of the main altar of Margam Abbey church. The centrepiece is one of the finest tombs in south Wales, raised in memory of Talbot's son **Theodore Mansel Talbot** (1839–76), a saintly character who dedicated his life to working among the slum-dwellers of London until his death following a hunting accident. Theodore's equally altruistic sister **Olivia Emma Talbot** (1842–94) was a great benefactress of the Church in Glamorgan and founded St Michael's Theological College, Llandaff. Talbot Street, Maesteg, until recently probably the only alcohol-free main street in Britain, is named after her, for she gave the land provided alcohol was never sold there. After 112 years this restrictive covenant was rescinded by the Bridgend magistrates to accommodate the needs of a local restaurant. To the right of the altar the Talbots' descendants by marriage, the **Mansels**, lie under some of the most outstanding Tudor and Jacobean tombs in the country.

NEATH

Born in Cornwall, **Joseph Tregelles Price** (1784–1854) took over his father's Neath Abbey ironworks in 1818 and made it into a highly prosperous enterprise, manufacturing a wide range of machinery but absolutely nothing that could be used in warfare. For Price was a committed Quaker, and in 1816 he became co-founder and first president of the Peace Society, an organization of which Henry Richard later became secretary. He ploughed an often lonely furrow in defence of his beliefs, and in the last year of his life he was forced to flee from a hostile crowd in his home town because of his unpopular stand against the Crimean War. A passionate humanitarian, Price was a patron of the movement to abolish slavery, and he played a prominent, but ultimately fruitless, part in the campaign to free Dic Penderyn, meeting both the Home Secretary and the Lord Chancellor. Notwithstanding George Borrow's observation that 'the Quakers are no friends to tombstones', the Friends' cemetery, where Price is buried, in the shadow of Neath castle, is well kept, the tombstones standing neatly in a row along the perimeter wall.

NEWPORT

BASSALEG
Buried in the family plot in the small northern section of St Basil's churchyard lies **Godfrey Charles Morgan**, **Viscount Tredegar** (1831–1913), the best-known and probably most popular member of one of the most influential families in the economic and social history of south Wales. While still Captain Morgan he took part in the charge of the Light Brigade at Balaclava in 1854; his trusty steed Sir Briggs, who also survived the ordeal, is buried in the garden of Tredegar House under a handsome obelisk. After serving for seventeen years as MP for Brecknock, Morgan succeeded his father as Baron Tredegar in 1875, becoming a viscount in 1905. Although he and his family were involved in the dramatic expansion of Cardiff and Newport (he became a freeman of both places in 1909), Lord Tredegar was personally, as well as politically, conservative by temperament, refusing to install either gas or electricity in his stately home, preferring good old candles and oil lamps. His statue, by Sir William Goscombe John, faces Cardiff City Hall. Near the church door, to the left of the main path, is the vault of another major south Wales dynasty, the Homfrays, including **Samuel George Homfray** (1830–94). The son of the managing partner of the Tredegar ironworks, he was for twenty years Deputy Provincial Grand Master of the Monmouthshire Freemasons. He was also an enthusiast for cricket, a sport he regarded as eminently suitable for men of his sort, and formed the South Wales Cricket Club in 1859, out of which, after several ups and downs, emerged the Glamorgan County Cricket Club in 1888. About forty yards to the left of the

Thomas Powell, Bassaleg

church door a Celtic cross marks the final resting place of **Thomas Powell** (1779– 1863), one of the giants of the south Wales coal industry who, at the time of his death, owned sixteen coal mines and was the greatest coal exporter in the world. Considering his importance, Powell's funeral was a remarkably low-key affair, the cortège consisting, according to the report in the *Cardiff and Merthyr Guardian* at the time, of 'the family and near relatives of the deceased and several of the agents of the concern'. It was not as if he had been living for several years in secluded retirement, for he had been to the office on the day before he died.

LLANWERN

David Alfred Thomas (1856–1918), Liberal MP for Merthyr Tydfil from 1888 to 1910, was Wales's greatest industrial magnate during the Edwardian period, building up a formidable industrial empire in coalmining, steel, the docks and railways and becoming a newspaper tycoon, owning the *Western Mail* and other Welsh papers. He also had fingers in several North American pies. During the bitter Cambrian collieries strike in 1911 Thomas became the most hated man in south Wales. In the First World War his undoubted administrative flair was recognized by his elevation to the peerage as Viscount Rhondda and his appointment, first as president of the Local Government Board and, in June 1917, as Food Controller, introducing food rationing and a whole range of other controls into everyday life. In fact he was lucky to be alive, for two years earlier he and his daughter had been among the survivors of the sinking of the *Lusitania*. The incident was reportedly greeted in one newspaper with the headline 'Great National Disaster. D. A. Thomas saved'. He is buried in Llanwern churchyard, to the right of the path leading to the church.

NEWPORT

The large St Woolos cemetery is the resting place of **Arthur Joseph Gould** (1864–1919), Welsh rugby union's first superstar. Playing at three-quarter he scored 554 points for Newport, including 136 tries (39 of them in 1892/3 alone), and played for Wales on 27 occasions, 18 of them as captain. He led Wales to their first Triple Crown in 1893. The end of his international career was controversial, for he was accused of professionalism by benefiting from the proceeds of a testimonial in 1897 which enabled him to buy his house. For a time, the row threatened to cause a permanent rift between Wales and the other home countries. 'The immortal Arthur Gould' died unexpectedly in January 1919, securing a handsome tribute from the *Daily Express*:

> Sure-footed, fast and the lucky owner of a bewildering swerve, he was a giant among giants.

His grave (block FCD 83, number 22), marked by a Celtic cross, is about 100 yards on the left of the path leading immediately to the left from the main entrance. **Mai Jones** (1899–1960), one of the great names of BBC radio light entertainment, lies in an unobtrusive grave, under her married name of **Gladys Mai Davies**, about 100 yards south-west of the chapel that stands to the left of the main entrance. She composed the music to Lyn Joshua's well-known song 'We'll keep a Welcome', first broadcast in 1940, and produced the popular light-entertainment programmes *Welsh Rarebit* and *Silver Chords*. She was credited with discovering Harry Secombe and Stan Stennett. She would call everybody 'Darling', to the annoyance of some. Towards the western end of the cemetery, near the grove of tall trees is the grave (section RC D31) of **Johnny Basham** (1890–1947), British welterweight boxing champion from 1914 to 1920 and, briefly, European middleweight champion in 1920. In later years he lived in sadly reduced circumstances, though his funeral was a grand affair. Not far away (in section CON D30) lies **Percy Blackborow** (1895–1949), a member of Sir Ernest Shackleton's nearly calamitous Antarctic expedition of 1914–16, having stowed aboard with his pet cat in Buenos Aires. When warned by an irate Shackleton that when expeditions ran out of food they always ate the stowaway first, 'Perce' is reported to have said that the crew would find a lot more meat on Shackleton than they would on him. As the youngest member of the expedition he was encouraged by Shackleton to be the first person ever to set foot on Elephant Island but, suffering severely from frostbite, he collapsed in the water and had to be helped ashore, where five toes were amputated from his left foot. He was given a hero's welcome on his return home, though he made little of his experiences in later life (as a local dock-worker) and managed to walk without limping. It is said that his wife only found out about his missing toes after their marriage.

The following memorial stands just inside the entrance to the churchyard of St Woolos Cathedral:

> On November 4th 1839 more than twenty supporters of the Chartist movement, which sought to establish democratic rights for all men, died in an exchange of shots at the Westgate Hotel, Newport. Ten were buried in this churchyard in unmarked graves. This stone is dedicated to their memory.

The ringleader of this challenge to the established order, business-man and one-time mayor of Newport, John Frost (1784–1877), fared rather better. Though initially sentenced to death this was commuted to transportation for life to Van Diemen's Land and, after a full pardon in 1856, he returned to Britain, spending his remaining years in Bristol.

PEMBROKESHIRE

CILGERRAN
Somewhere in the church are the remains of **Thomas Phaer** (1510?–60), lawyer, physician and scholar, who was the author of the first work in English on childcare, *The Boke of Chyldren* (1544). In it he proposed all sorts of remedies for a wide range of children's disorders, from squinting to 'pissing in the bedde'. He was a firm be-liever in the benefits of breastfeeding, ideally by the natural mother:

> If not ye must be well advised in taking of a nource, not of ill complexion and of worse manners; but such as be sobre, honeste and chaste, well formed, amiable and chearefull.

His actual burial place is no longer known, the stone marking the spot probably having been disturbed during renovation work carried out in the early nineteenth century (such vandalism being common-place in those days). However, a plaque was erected to his memory in the church on Mothering Sunday 1986, in the presence of the bishop of St Davids, the president of the British Paediatric Society and various luminaries from the University of Wales College of Medicine and the Welsh History of Medicine Society. The plaque quotes Phaer's purpose in writing his book:

> To do them good that have most need,
> that is to say children;
> and to shew the remedies
> that God hath created for the use of man.

FISHGUARD

Fishguard is famous as the place where the last foreign invasion of the British mainland occurred, in 1797, when French troops landed in west Wales with the intention of providing a diversion while the main French forces invaded Ireland. The plan was a hopeless failure, the hapless troops surrendering to Lord Cawdor after three days. One of the best-known incidents during this brief conflict involved a beefy local cobbler, **Jemima Nicholas** (*c.*1750–1832) who single-handed, armed only with a pitchfork, rounded up twelve French soldiers and brought them back to town. She became a local celebrity, and was awarded an annual pension of fifty pounds by the government. Her resting place in St Mary's churchyard is no longer known, but near the church door stands a memorial stone to:

> the Welsh heroine who boldly marched to meet the French invaders who landed on our shores in February 1797.

LLANDYSILIO

Although he published only one book of poetry, *Dail Pren*, **Waldo Williams** (1904–71) is widely revered as one of the most distinguished Welsh poets of the twentieth century, and attractive posters carrying one of his best-known poems, 'Cofio', adorn the walls of studies, student bedrooms and cafés all over Wales. He was an ardent Welsh nationalist and pacifist who once, reluctantly, stood for Parliament for Plaid Cymru, and twice went to jail for refusing to pay his income tax while conscription to the armed forces continued. His gravestone, in the middle of Blaenconin Baptist chapel cemetery, near the back (and right on the boundary with Carmarthenshire), bears the verse 'Gwyn eu byd y tangnefeddwyr' (Blessed are the peacemakers). He is also commemorated by a memorial stone raised on common land just outside Mynachlog-ddu, where he had lived as a boy.

MILFORD HAVEN

In 1793 some Quaker whaling families from Nantucket, unwelcome in the new United States of America because of their neutrality during the American War of Independence, settled in Milford Haven, where they prospered. Adjoining the small Friends' meeting house, which is still used today, is a cemetery where they and their descendants are buried. The simplicity of their faith is reflected in the simplicity of the headstones, bearing just initials and the year of burial.

MYNACHLOG-DDU

The Rebecca riots, which took place in south-west Wales on and off between 1839 and 1843, never had an overall leader; each scattered disturbance had its own leaders, often dressed as women as a form of disguise. However **Thomas Rees** (1806?–76), an independent-minded agricultural labourer, is acknowledged as a leading participant in the first recorded Rebecca riot, in the summer of 1839, when the toll-gate at Efailwen, on the Carmarthenshire/Pembrokeshire border, was attacked. Nothing seems to have happened to Rees after this incident and (known as **Twm Carnabwth** after the name of his farmhouse) he pursued a successful career as a pugilist until 1847, when he lost an eye in a drunken brawl. Thereafter, Rees turned over a new leaf, becoming a pillar of the local Baptist chapel at Mynachlog-ddu. His grave is on the right of the cemetery, in the back row, and the headstone carries a rather poignant Welsh epitaph which, when translated into English, reads:

> No one but God knows
> What may happen in a day.
> While fetching a cabbage for my dinner
> Death came into my garden and struck me.

To the left of the chapel lies a popular local poet **William Rees Evans** (1910–91), known as **Wil Glynsaithmaen**. On his rough stone headstone is an affectionate tribute by the celebrated poet Dic Jones:

> Ond ma'i haul e'n dwym o hyd—in gifoth
>   O atgofion hifryd,
> Ma'r Nef yn wherthin hefyd
> Lle buo' Wil ma' gwell byd.

William Rees Evans,
Mynachlog-ddu

(His sun still warms us with a wealth
Of sweet memories.
There is laughter as well in Paradise,
Heaven and Earth are enhanced by Wil's
    presence.)

NARBERTH

Parc Gwyn crematorium has been the end of the road for many notable Welshmen over the years. The ashes of some, such as Sir Geraint Evans and Professor Gwyn Alf Williams, have been buried elsewhere. The ashes of Thomas Evan Nicholas (1878–1971), Niclas y Glais, poet, preacher, Communist pioneer – and dentist – once hailed by Harry Pollitt as 'Wales's greatest man', were scattered on the Preseli hills where he had been born. Those of the celebrated journalist, broadcaster and raconteur Wynford Vaughan-Thomas (1908–87) were scattered privately by his family.

NEVERN

On the wall near to the pulpit inside the ancient St Brynach's church is a plaque 'To the Glory of God and to the famous memory' of **George Owen of Henllys** (*c.*1552–1613) who is buried nearby. He was one of the greatest antiquarians of his day, best known for his assiduously researched *Description of Penbrockshire*, completed in 1603, and, a proud son of that county, had taken umbrage at the highly unflattering descriptions of the condition of Wales written by the extreme Puritan John Penry, certainly as far as his beloved native county was concerned. Outside, at the eastern end of the churchyard, lies **John Jones** (1792–1852), better known as **Ioan Tegid**, scholar, vicar of the church for the last ten years of his life, and one of the translators of the notorious 'Blue Books' into Welsh.

ST DAVID'S

It is believed that three of Wales's greatest national heroes are buried in St Davids Cathedral. Not very much is known about **Dewi Sant** or **St David** (*c.*520–*c.*588), patron saint of Wales, though he did establish a monastery in the area of the present St Davids, using it as the hub of a network of monasteries he set up in west Wales during the sixth century. Monastic life under Dewi was extremely spartan, combining hard work and earnest contemplation, nourished by little

89

more than bread and water (he was known as 'Dewi Ddyfrwr' – the water drinker), but his asceticism and concern for the poor were much admired. Greatly mourned when he died, tradition has it that he was buried on the site of the present St Davids Cathedral (built in 1188) though no one now believes that his remains are still preserved in the reliquary behind the main altar. **Rhys ap Gruffudd** (1132–97), the youngest son of the Welsh heroine Gwenllïan, is certainly buried

Rhys ap Gruffudd, St Davids Cathedral

in the cathedral, his resting place in the south choir aisle being marked by a fine stone effigy. Generally known as **the Lord Rhys**, ruler of Deheubarth, he was the outstanding native Welsh leader during the latter part of the twelfth century and, a great patriot, he was responsible for convening what is now recognized as Wales's first National Eisteddfod in Cardigan in 1176. Next to his effigy is one thought to be that of Rhys's kinsman **Gerald of Wales** (1146?–1223), one of the most remarkable products of medieval Wales. Scholar, churchman, traveller, writer and patriot, his greatest achievement was as the outstanding chronicler of Welsh life during the Middle Ages, demonstrating vividly in his most celebrated works *Journey through Wales* and *A Description of Wales* the extent to which there was a distinct Welsh community at the end of the twelfth century. In his words:

> The Welsh are extreme in all they do; so that if you never meet anyone worse than a bad Welshman, you will never meet anyone better than a good one.

For a few years Gerald fought an ultimately fruitless campaign to obtain the independence of the Welsh Church from Canterbury, with himself as archbishop. He spent the last years of his life in Lincoln, a disappointed man, but after his death he was, reputedly, buried in St Davids Cathedral. **Edmund Tudor** (*c*.1430–56), son of Catherine de Valois, Henry V's widow, was a man of no particular distinction himself but he did marry Margaret Beaufort, a great-great-granddaughter of Edward III, and their son, Henry Tudor, born in Pembroke castle three months after Edmund's premature death, became King Henry VII. Edmund was buried at Greyfriars, Carmarthen, but in 1536, at the time of the dissolution of the monasteries, his remains were reburied in St Davids Cathedral under an imposing chest-tomb in front of the altar.

STACKPOLE ELIDOR
In the churchyard lies **Frederick Archibald Vaughan Campbell**, **3rd Earl Cawdor** (1847–1911), Conservative MP for Carmarthen 1874–85, a member of the Aberdare Commission into Intermediate and Higher Education in Wales, and chairman of the Great Western Railway from 1895 until 1905, when he became First Lord of the Admiralty in the dying months of Balfour's Conservative government. He was a leading opponent of Lloyd George's 1909 budget, accusing the Liberal government of 'denying socialism in words but putting socialism in their budget'. He was one of the four Conservative representatives (with Balfour, Lansdowne and Austen Chamberlain) at the fruitless constitutional conference convened in 1910 to try to resolve the impasse between the Lords and the Commons. After his death in the following year he was buried in an ordinary grave at the upper end of the churchyard, having expressed an objection, three years earlier, to being put in the family vault, preferring to be buried 'earth to earth'.

POWYS (BRECONSHIRE)

ABERCRAVE
As part of the Millennium celebrations a caveman was buried in October 1999, within a specially constructed stone circle at the site of the National Showcaves of Wales. The caveman's remains had originally been found in one of the Dan yr Ogof caves in 1943, and he is thought to have been a member of a small farming community

about 3,000 years ago who had probably been killed in a battle with a rival tribe. He was buried, near the car park, in a box draped with a Welsh flag, but much to the dismay of the local Celtic pagan group, Isis Briganta, the caveman was subjected to a Christian burial service, performed by a Church in Wales minister. As a spokesman for the group solemnly told the *Western Mail*:

> This is an insult to pagan worshippers everywhere. It is not the place of one generation to inflict its religious views on another. I would hate to think that someone who found my remains in 3,000 years' time would take it on themselves to call me a Christian.

BRECON

In the north-east corner of Brecon Cathedral churchyard is the elegant tomb of **Charles Henry Lumley** (1824–58), a captain in the 97th (Earl of Ulster's) Regiment who was awarded the Victoria Cross for bravery at the assault of the Redan, Sebastopol in 1857, in the Crimean War, during which, according to the citation, he received 'a ball in the mouth which wounded him most severely'. Though personally decorated with the VC by Queen Victoria and promoted to the rank of major, he shot himself in the head at Brecon in the following year because, according to the subsequent inquest, of 'temporary insanity'.

CWM-DU

Nowadays known mainly as a friend of Lady Llanover and the possessor of a seemingly unpronounceable bardic name **Carnhuanawc**, the **Reverend Thomas Price** (1787–1848) deserves recognition as (in John Davies's words) 'one of the great Welshmen of the nineteenth century'. He spent much of his adult life as a curate in parishes in the Crickhowell area, from where he launched his campaign to instil in his compatriots a love for their language and heritage. With the patronage of Lady Llanover he launched, in 1834, Cymdeithas Cymreigyddion y Fenni ('the Abergavenny society of Welsh scholars'), making the Abergavenny area the hot-bed of Welsh cultural life for some years. He was involved in the establishment of the Welsh Manuscripts Society and, a leading figure in the pan-Celtic movement at that time, collaborated in the translation of the Bible into Breton. His greatest achievement was his *Hanes Cymru* (History of Wales, from earliest times to the death of Llywelyn ap Gruffudd), appearing first in instalments in the 1830s, then as a book in 1842. He is buried in the north side of the

Carnhuanawc, Cwm-du

churchyard at Llanfihangel Cwm-du where he was vicar from 1825, his tombstone recently having been given a new commemorative plaque by the Cymdeithas Carnhuanawc Society.

LLANGAMARCH WELLS
Theophilus Evans (1693–1767), rector of the parish for twenty-five years, was a celebrated historian whose mission was to glorify the Welsh nation. In his best-known and most influential work, *Drych y Prif Oesoedd* (the Mirror of the First Ages) (1716, 1740), using whatever sources were most convenient for his purposes, including Geoffrey of Monmouth's somewhat fanciful *History of the Kings of Britain*, he demonstrated that the Welsh could trace their august ancestry back to the ancient Hebrews, from Gomer, son of Japheth, son of Noah himself. Theophilus Evans is also credited with the discovery, in 1732, of the healing properties of the waters at Llanwrtyd Wells, which apparently cured him of scurvy. He is buried next to the gate at the east end of the churchyard, under a now virtually indecipherable tombstone. Despite the wording on a commemorative plaque inside the church, it is believed that his grave also contains the body of his grandson **Theophilus Jones** (1759–1812), author of the pioneering two-volume *History of the County of Brecknock* (1805, 1809). In the churchyard, overlooking the road, stands a modern statue by the local sculptor Elizabeth Yeomans of John Penry (1563–93), Wales's first Puritan martyr, who was born in the parish and became a thorn in the flesh of Elizabethan England. The plaque reads:

> He campaigned for a Welsh Bible
> And preaching in Welsh,
> He was hanged as a Puritan.

LLANGASTY
A fine headstone in the north-east section of Llangasty churchyard, overlooking Llangorse lake, marks the grave of **Sir Thomas Lewis** (1881–1945), a Cardiff man who became one of the world's leaders in the field of cardiology and who laid the foundation of modern electrocardiography. His work on the effect of stress on the circulatory systems of fighting men during the First World War ('soldiers' heart') earned him a knighthood. The Chair of Cardiology at the University of Wales College of Medicine is named after him, though his professional life was mainly spent in London. In 1981, on the centenary of his birth, Mauritius, whose prime minister had once

studied under Lewis, issued a postage stamp in his memory, depicting his portrait and his pioneering electrocardiograph.

LLANSANFFRAID

At the top end of the churchyard (he felt unworthy to be buried inside the church) is the well-signposted grave of the great metaphysical poet **Henry Vaughan** (1621–95). His greatest work, *Silex*

Henry Vaughan, Llansanffraid

Scintillans (1650), a deeply religious collection, includes such memorable poems as 'Peace' ('My Soul, there is a Countrie') and 'The World' ('I saw Eternity the other night'). Vaughan adopted the title 'Silurian' to denote his identity with his home district, an area where the Silures, a fiercely independent British tribe, had once resisted the Roman invaders; no doubt, as a staunch royalist, he was also signalling his distaste for the new Cromwellian regime. Vaughan is probably best remembered today as the subject of a well-known poem, 'At the grave of Henry Vaughan', by Siegfried Sassoon. The epitaph on the gravestone, composed by Vaughan, reads:

Hic iacet Henricus Vaughan, Siluris, servus inutilis, peccator maximus

(Here lies Henry Vaughan, Silurian, useless servant, greatest of sinners)

TALGARTH

If Daniel Rowland was the orator of the Welsh Methodist revival of the eighteenth century and William Williams, Pantycelyn, was the hymn-writer, **Howel Harris** (1714–73), the schoolteacher son of a prosperous farmer, was the inspired organizer. He experienced a dramatic conversion in 1735 and, prevented from becoming an ordained clergyman because of his excessive zeal, he journeyed the length and breadth of Wales, preaching to huge crowds. He established local societies of Methodists, mainly in the more receptive south (according to him, the people in the north had 'poor, silly minds') but, an arrogant man, he fell out with Rowland and other leading reformers and withdrew from the stage in 1752 to set up a quasi-monastic community in his birthplace, Trefeca. Here he pioneered some of the agricultural innovations of the period and, in 1755, was co-founder of the Brecknockshire Agricultural Society, the first of its kind in Wales. Though he never regained the leadership of the Methodist movement, there were said to be over 20,000 people at St Gwendoline's church, Talgarth, for his funeral. The commemorative tablet marking his burial place near the communion table harks back to the time of his conversion in 1735:

> Here where his body lies, he was convinced of sin, had his pardon sealed, felt the power of Christ's precious blood at Holy Communion.

POWYS (MONTGOMERYSHIRE)

CARNO

About fifty yards beyond the back of the church of St John the Baptist is the simple grave of **Laura Ashley** (1925–85) who, with her husband, established a major fashion enterprise which spread the 'Made in Wales' label throughout the world. Sadly, at the height of her career, she died in an accident at her daughter's Cotswolds home, but it was entirely fitting that she should be buried in the mid-Wales village which had become the centre of her empire, borne to her grave to the sound of the Dowlais Male Voice Choir, of which, as a Dowlais girl herself, she had been proud to be Vice-President. Her birthplace, 31 Station Terrace, Dowlais Top, now displays a commemorative plaque.

CEMAIS
Priest and scholar, and, appointed part-time professor of Welsh at University College of Wales, Aberystwyth in 1874, the world's first professor of Welsh, **Daniel Silvan Evans** (1818–1903) is best remembered as the man who aspired to produce the Welsh equivalent of the *Oxford English Dictionary*. This project dominated the last quarter of his life and brought him much recognition, including an honorary doctorate from the University of Wales. Unfortunately he never finished the task. He always had too many irons in the fire at any one time and, by the time of his death, he had managed to publish only four volumes of *Y Geiriadur Cymraeg* with a fifth appearing posthumously, taking the project as far as 'E'. He is buried to the right of the path leading from the churchyard gate, under a large yew tree.

LEIGHTON
John Naylor (1813–89), a wealthy Liverpool banker, was given the Leighton estate, across the valley from Welshpool, in 1846 as a wedding present from his uncle and, like many others in his position at that time, he proceeded to lavish much of his fortune on the development of his fiefdom. He built Leighton Hall, still a handsome Gothic edifice, and nearby Holy Trinity church with a spire that can be seen for miles. Naylor was a highly innovative landowner. His farm buildings, as well as the hall and the church, were all lit by gas produced by his own gasworks. His greatest agricultural achievement was the construction, at the top of Moel y Mab, of a tank filled with manure from his cowsheds which fertilized the fields below via a system of pipes, the flow controlled by brass taps. On his estate was grown the original of the Leyland cypress, named after Naylor's bank, and now, in John Davies's words, 'the great menace of suburbia' (*The Making of Wales*, 1996). He rests in the family vault in the vicinity of a splendid octagonal chapel at the south-east corner of the church. The elegant mausoleum is filled with memorials of the family and is dominated by a fine stone carving of an angel undertaken by Naylor's fourth daughter.

LLANBRYN-MAIR
Under his bardic name **Mynyddog**, **Richard Davies** (1833–77) was a

popular *eisteddfodwr*, as a competitor and an adjudicator, and wrote the not particularly distinguished libretto for Joseph Parry's opera *Blodwen*. Some of the lines of Davies's poem 'Rheolau'r Aelwyd', which appeared in his third collection of poems published in 1877, some years later became the first verse of Llanelli's own anthem, 'Sospan Fach'. An obelisk marking his grave is adjacent to the house adjoining the historic Hen Gapel. After his death his widow married the composer David Emlyn Evans.

LLANDINAM
David Davies (1818–90) rose, by ruthless determination and hard work, from rural obscurity to become Wales's first industrial tycoon. He pioneered railway development into many parts of Wales, he became one of the largest mine owners in south Wales, and built Barry docks as an outlet for his coal. A strict Non-conformist, he tried (but failed) to curtail the opening hours of public houses to ensure a sober workforce and he would do no work on the Lord's Day, not even open letters. He was Liberal MP for Cardigan Boroughs from 1874 to 1885 and for Cardiganshire 1885–6, and he had the irritating habit of referring to himself with obvious approval as a self-made man, once earning this dry observation from Disraeli: 'I am glad to hear the Honourable Member praising his creator.' He is buried in the north-east section of the churchyard. His epitaph sums up his approach to life very well:

> Whatever thy hand findeth to do,
> do it with thy might.

(Ecclesiastes 9:10)

LLANFIHANGEL-YNG-NGWYNFA
Under a substantial obelisk on the left of the path leading to the church door lies **Ann Griffiths** (1776–1805), ranked among Wales's greatest religious poets. She lived all of her short life (she died in childbirth) at nearby Dolwar-fach and, having experienced a conversion in 1796, spent the rest of her days composing verse of great power in praise of God. She never wrote any of it down, but fortunately Ruth Evans, an illiterate maid in her household, managed to memorize the poems and related them to her husband, the eminent preacher, John Hughes, Pontrobert. He did write them down, thereby preserving for posterity some of the finest verse in the Welsh language. Ann Griffiths's best-loved composition is 'Wele'n

sefyll rhwng y myrtwydd' (Lo, between the myrtles standing), usually sung with gusto to the tune 'Cwm Rhondda'.

LLANGEDWYN

Across the road from the family home is Llangedwyn church, in the graveyard of which lie several generations of the Williams Wynn dynasty, from the nineteenth century to the present day. Prominent among them was the 6th baronet, **Sir Watkin Williams Wynn** (1820–85), MP for Denbighshire from 1841 until his defeat in 1885, heralding the end of the family's dominance over Denbighshire politics which had lasted for 169 years. His grave is located in the south-eastern section of the churchyard.

LLANSILIN

A squire in Dyffryn Ceiriog, **Huw Morys** (1622–1709) is regarded as the most prolific and gifted Welsh poet of the seventeenth century, taking a strong anti-Puritan stance. Known as **Eos Ceiriog**, his 'ranting roaring verses against the Roundheads' were admired by George Borrow for their vigour if not their sentiments, and Borrow's pilgrimage to Morys's grave in Llansilin churchyard, by the north wall of the church, is described in *Wild Wales*: 'I went down on my knees and kissed the cold slab covering the cold remains of the mighty Huw.'

LLANWNOG

Brought up in Llanarmon in the Ceiriog valley, **John Ceiriog Hughes** (1832–87) rose from being a farmhand and a clerk in a Manchester railway goods office to becoming the station-master at Llanidloes. In the 1870s he was manager of the Van Railway, the last railway line built by David Davies, Llandinam. This six-mile stretch of track linked the lead mine at Van, in its heyday the largest lead mine in Britain, to the main Newtown– Machynlleth line at Caersws. Modest though this line was, many people travelled

Ceiriog, Llanwnog

99

along it purely in order to meet and converse with Hughes for, though rather eccentric, he was one of Wales's most celebrated bards. Taking the name **Ceiriog**, he gained a reputation as the Robert Burns of Wales and among his best-known compositions are the words of 'Men of Harlech', 'God Bless the Prince of Wales' and 'David of the White Rock'. His grave, in Llanwnog church-yard, near Caersws, is well signposted, and bears his own epitaph:

> Carodd eiriau cerddorol,—carodd feirdd,
>   Carodd fyw'n naturiol;
>   Carodd gerdd yn angerddol:
> Dyma ei lwch,—a dim lol.

> (He loved musical words, he loved poets,
> He loved to live naturally;
> He loved poetry passionately;
> Here is his dust, and no nonsense.)

MACHYNLLETH

No one knows for certain when or where Wales's greatest national hero, Owain Glyndŵr (1359?–1415?) died, though it is now generally thought that he probably died at the home of his daughter at Monnington Straddel in Herefordshire, now Monnington Court farm, near Vowchurch, and is buried there somewhere. The Owain Glyndŵr Society is committed to finding the grave. Meanwhile, the society has taken the lead in erecting a handsome slate memorial to Owain outside the entrance to the tourist attraction Celtica in Machynlleth, the town where Owain convened the first Welsh parliament in 1404.

MEIFOD

Born in Llanfyllin, **Clement Edward Davies** (1884–1962) became Liberal MP for his native county in 1929. As a Liberal National during the 1930s, he gave general support to the National govern-ments of the day but became an outspoken and influential advocate of Neville Chamberlain's replacement by Churchill in 1940. His friend Lord Boothby later referred to Davies as 'one of the architects of the advent to power of Churchill'. By the time of the 1945 general election Davies had rejoined the mainstream of the Liberal Party, or what was left of it, and between 1945 and 1956 he served as leader of the Liberals in the House of Commons, during the party's leanest years. After the 1951 general election, when Liberal representation had been reduced to six, Churchill offered Davies a seat in the Cabinet as Minister of Education but, though he rather liked the idea, the Liberal grandees would have nothing of it. So Davies soldiered on until 1956 when he was finally persuaded to stand down. He continued as an MP until his death. He is buried in the south-east corner of the churchyard.

MONTGOMERY
John Davies, a plasterer, was found guilty of robbery on the Welshpool to Newtown highway, a crime for which he was hanged at Montgomery in September 1821. Proclaiming his innocence to the end he prophesied that God would not allow grass to grow on his grave, and it is said that at the moment of his execution a fierce storm broke over the town. A wooden cross carrying the words 'Robber's Grave' and a rose bush mark the spot near to the north gate of St Nicholas's churchyard where John Davies is reputed to have been buried. Though the spot is no longer conspicuously bare, tradition has it that it had been so well into the twentieth century. Also buried in the churchyard, near to the western perimeter, is **Geraint Goodwin** (1903–41), a popular storyteller and novelist between the wars, remembered for his depiction of life in the Welsh border communities.

NEWTOWN
In old St Mary's churchyard, within elaborate wrought-iron railings, is one of Wales's most visited graves, that of the socialist pioneer **Robert Owen** (1771–1858), who returned to his native town to die, after spending most of his life making the established order anxious. He took the view that employers could treat working people decently and still make a profit, and he tried to practise what he preached in his New Lanark mills in Scotland. His philosophy was set out in his influential *A New View of Society* (1813), which was widely regarded as a threat to the status quo; however, his efforts to promote trade unionism came to nothing in the short term. Though he dabbled in spiritualism towards the end of his life (apparently making contact with people like Thomas Jefferson) he was fundamentally a rationalist, and much offence was caused when he was given a Christian funeral.

Across the river in Llanllwchaiarn churchyard, just to the right of the entrance, is an obelisk marking the grave of **Sir Pryce Pryce-Jones** (1834–1920), a local wool manufacturer who set up the first mail-order business in the world. As his order books expanded so did his premises, the Royal Welsh Warehouse, and by the 1880s the London and North-Western Railway Company was providing three specially designed carriages to transport the firm's products to London, dropping off parcels on the way. Queen Victoria (who knighted him in 1887) and the other crowned heads of Europe were regular customers, and his most famous invention, the 'Eukalisia', a combination of rug, shawl and inflatable pillow, was much appreciated by the German army during the Franco-Prussian war. He is believed to have been the first person in Wales to install a telephone system, linking his mansion, Dolerw, to his business in town, in 1878. He was also instrumental in the setting up of the parcel-post system in the 1880s. For some years he served as Conservative MP for Montgomery Boroughs. His warehouse, now owned by another mail-order business, Kays of Worcester, still dominates the town.

POWYS (RADNORSHIRE)

CAPEL-Y-FFIN
Joseph Leycester Lyne (1837–1908) was a controversial figure on the outer fringes of Victorian Anglicanism. Generally known as **Father Ignatius**, he sought to introduce Benedictine monasticism in the Church of England, establishing a monastery at a remote spot near to Llanthony abbey. Though admired by Francis Kilvert as a man of 'great earnestness and singlemindedness', Lyne was an eccentric character who had questionable ways of raising funds, dabbled with miracles and consorted with bogus clerics. During a visit to the United States, where he preached to the Sioux Indians, he became convinced that the earth was flat, the circumference surrounded by ice to prevent the seas from pouring away. At the Brecon National Eisteddfod of 1889, best known for Adelina Patti's storming performance, Lyne became a druid with the bardic name Dewi Honddu. The monastery at Capel-y-ffin did not long survive his death, though his grave, in the monastery, is still maintained by the Father Ignatius Memorial Trust.

CWM-HIR
The trunk of **Llywelyn ap Gruffudd** (died 1282) is believed to lie in this ruined Cistercian abbey, near to where the altar once stood, and a modern stone slab marks the presumed burial spot. After his

murder, near Cilmeri, his head was taken first to Edward I in north Wales and then to London, where it was displayed around the streets; for Edward was very keen to demonstrate that Llywelyn, the last authentic Prince of Wales, acknowledged as such by King Henry III in 1267, and a thorn in the English flesh, was indeed dead. The Welsh bards were inconsolable, as demonstrated in Gruffudd ab yr Ynad Goch's powerful ode:

> Och hyd atat ti Dduw na ddaw— môr dros dir!
> Pa beth y'n gedir i ohiriaw?
>
> (O God, why does not the sea cover the land?
> Why are we left to linger?)

LLANBEDR

For the last thirty-six years of his life **John Price** (1810–95), a learned and sensitive clergyman, eked out a meagre living as vicar at Llanbedr, residing in awful makeshift accommodation. In his diary of 3 July 1872, Francis Kilvert recorded that 'the squalor, the dirt, the dust, the foulness and wretchedness of the place were indescribable, almost inconceivable'. Perhaps because of his own dire straits Price, known as the 'tramps' chaplain', had a particularly soft spot for vagrants, who used to flock to his Sunday morning services for handouts, grossly abusing his good-natured generosity and his failing eyesight. Despite everything, the local parishioners thought the world of him. According to Kilvert:

> they recognized him as a very holy man and if the Solitary had lived a thousand years ago he would have been revered as a hermit and perhaps canonized as a Saint.

At least the last few days of this lonely old man's life were spent between clean sheets in a comfortable bed in Talgarth. His grave, marked by a white stone cross, is in the west of the churchyard.

LLANDRINDOD WELLS

On the left of the entrance to the old parish churchyard lies **Tom Norton** (1870–1955), transport pioneer and friend of Henry Ford. Starting in 1899 with the first Raleigh depot in Wales, by the time of the First World War he had opened the historic art deco Palace of Sport (with distinctive white faience, or glazed tiles) which served as the first Ford agency in Wales and the base for one of the first public bus services, from Llandrindod Wells to Newtown. Renamed the

Automobile Palace in 1925, the building now houses the National Cycle Exhibition. In 1949, Norton became the president of the Fellowship of Old Time Cyclists, a club restricted to those born before 1873 and who had ridden a penny-farthing before the age of seventeen.

NEWBRIDGE-ON-WYE
George Stovin Venables (1810–88), who broke William Makepeace Thackeray's nose at Charterhouse school, became a highly successful barrister with such a good memory that he was reputed never to use a note in court. He was a regular contributor to the weekly journal, the *Saturday Review*, for over thirty years, and for twenty-five years wrote the annual review of events which appeared in *The Times* on the last day of the year. He was a friend of Francis Kilvert and would send him pheasants and rabbits from time to time. He is buried in the family plot behind a neat hedge on the west side of the churchyard, and the brown marble coping-stone covering his grave describes him as 'founder of this church'.

NORTON
Sir Richard Green-Price (1803–87), Liberal MP for Radnor Boroughs from 1863 to 1869 and for Radnorshire from 1880 to 1885, was the man primarily responsible for developing the Central Wales railway line between Craven Arms and Llandovery and, as part of his plan to develop mid-Victorian Presteigne, he established a branch line to the town in 1875. He transformed the village of Norton, having the church restored by Sir Gilbert Scott. He is buried under a Celtic cross in the north-west of the churchyard.

PILLETH

The grove of trees at Pilleth

About six miles west of Presteigne, to the right of the B4356, on the hillside above the ancient church of Our Lady of Pilleth, is a distinctive grove of four tall Wellingtonia fir trees enclosed in a small field. These trees, planted by Sir Richard Green-Price, mark the burial place of hundreds of English soldiers killed by the army of Owain Glyndŵr at the battle of Bryn Glas on St Alban's Day,

22 June 1402. Relying on the prejudiced account of the Tudor historian and propagandist Holinshed, Shakespeare described the battle thus in *Henry IV Part I*:

> . . . the noble Mortimer
> Leading the men of Hereford to fight
> Against the irregular and wild Glendower,
> Was by the rude hands of that Welshman taken;
> A thousand of his people butchered,
> Upon whose dead corpse there was such misuse,
> Such beastly, shameless, transformation
> By those Welsh women done, as may not be,
> Without much shame, retold or spoken of.

In the churchyard itself, Sir Richard placed a rectangular kerbstone marking the location where other English soldiers were buried. Some of the descendants of Sir Richard Green-Price, including the third and fourth baronets, are buried in Pilleth churchyard.

PRESTEIGNE

Mary Morgan (1788–1805), an under-cook at the home of Walter Wilkins, the local MP, gave birth in September 1804 to an illegitimate baby girl whom she promptly killed with a kitchen knife. Found guilty of infanticide, she was executed at Gallows Lane, Presteigne in April 1805, shortly after her seventeenth birthday, thereby holding the record as the last woman in Wales to be publicly executed. Though her general attitude in court probably did for her, she elicited much local sympathy, and a few years after her death her burial place, in what was then unconsecrated ground in the south-west of St Andrew's parish churchyard,

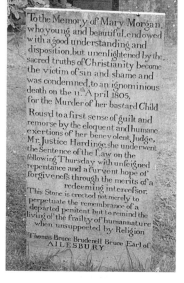

was marked with a headstone carrying the inscription: 'He that is without sin amongst you / Let him first cast a stone at her.' Close by is another, rather more pious headstone, erected by the Earl of Ailesbury, a friend of the judge who sentenced Mary to death, which ends:

> This stone is erected not merely to perpetuate the remembrance of a departed penitent, but to remind the living of the frailty of human nature when unsupported by Religion.

RHONDDA CYNON TAF

ABERDARE

According to the memorial to the left of the west door of St John's church **David William Watkins** (died 1789), a Quaker from Aberaman, was buried 'perpendicularly beneath this tablet'. In other words, according to popular belief, he was buried standing upright, some say so that he would be well placed to make a speedy response to the sound of the Last Trumpet. The churchyard was substantially landscaped in 1972, with many of the gravestones relocated around the perimeter wall. Near the west wall is a nicely carved gravestone with a rather touching epitaph: 'This stone is designed to rescue from oblivion the memory of **Joseph Hyat Parfitt**, late organist of St Elvan's church,' who died in 1858 aged forty. Nearby is an elegant memorial erected by Griffith Rhys Jones (Caradog) to his wife, his parents and grandparents.

A little way down from the main entrance of Aberdare cemetery (plot number H 3/18) is a now rather battered Celtic cross marking the grave of **David Williams** (1809–63), a major figure in the National Eisteddfod movement during the mid-nineteenth century, known by his bardic name **Alaw Goch**. He was one of the wealthiest coalowners in the south Wales valleys, and Trealaw, the mining community in the Rhondda valley, was named after him. Just to the right of the main entrance, in section B (plot number L 25/4) is the grave of **James James** (1833–1902), publican and talented harpist who composed the tune to 'Hen Wlad fy Nhadau'. Which came first, his father's words or the music, remains a matter of dispute to this day. There is, however, general agreement that most of the composition was put together one Sunday in January 1856 and that James was told off by his mother for playing the harp on the Sabbath. **Griffith Rhys Jones** (1834–97), known to all as **Caradog**, was the most celebrated choral conductor of his day. He is credited with coining the phrase 'Wales, the Land of Song' in 1878. His greatest achievement was as the conductor of the South Wales Choral Union ('Côr Caradog') which won the Crystal Palace Challenge Trophy in 1872 and 1873, victories which did much to heighten the self-esteem of Welsh people at the time. The handsome trophy is now displayed in the Museum of Welsh Life. Caradog's splendid tomb (plot number W 8/17), his face carved in bas-relief at the front,

is in section R, on the right, some way along the path which skirts the cemetery's northern perimeter. His statue, by Sir William Goscombe John, was unveiled in Victoria Square, Aberdare in July 1920, the ceremony being attended by over 120 of his former choristers. Not far from Caradog (in section C, plot number E 6/16) lies **Arthur Linton** (1868–96), the greatest Welsh cyclist of his era. In 1893 Linton broke all the Welsh cycling records from five to twenty-two miles; in 1894 he broke four world records and was crowned Champion Cyclist of the World in 1895/6. Shortly after controversially tying for first place in the 1896 Bordeaux to Paris cycle race, the blue riband event in professional cycling, he died suddenly. The cause was officially ascribed to typhoid fever though it was rumoured at the time that his premature death had been brought on by illegal drugs administered by his trainer, Linton's demise thereby representing the first death induced by drug abuse in modern sporting history. Whatever the cause, Linton's death came as a great shock to the local community and his funeral was one of the largest ever seen in Aberdare, with his favourite cycle, draped in crêpe, being pushed behind the cortège by one of his French rivals. The name on his brown marble obelisk is spelt 'Lenton' for some reason.

CHURCH VILLAGE

John Hughes (1873–1932), who worked for most of his life as a miner, then a railway official, was a talented musician who composed one of the best-known hymn tunes in the world, 'Cwm Rhondda', in 1907 for a *cymanfa ganu* at Rhondda Baptist chapel, Hopkinstown. In fact, the tune was originally named 'Rhondda' after the chapel where it was first heard but Hughes later changed the title to 'Cwm Rhondda' to avoid confusion with another hymn named 'Rhondda'. He is buried in the graveyard of Salem Baptist chapel where he was a deacon. His grave may be found by walking up the path by the side of the chapel and taking the first turning to the left. The grave is about twenty-five yards along on the right-hand side.

CYMER

In the distressingly neglected cemetery adjoining the historic, but now derelict, Independent chapel lies **Daniel Thomas** (1849–84), the central figure in one of the most dramatic mining rescues of the late nineteenth century. In April 1877, several miners were trapped underground in the Tynewydd colliery near Porth, following a flood from old workings in the adjoining Cymer colliery. Although only five miners were killed and five rescued after nine days under-ground, the incident caught the public imagination and the Home Secretary gave progress reports to the House of Commons. Until the Tynewydd disaster the Albert Medal, the forerunner of the George Cross, had been awarded only for bravery at sea. However, Queen Victoria announced that the Albert Medal

> shall be extended to similar actions on land, and that the first medals struck for this purpose shall be conferred on the heroic rescuers of the Welsh miners.

Daniel Thomas, the leader of the rescue team, and three others were awarded the Albert Medal of the First Class. The gallant Daniel Thomas was killed by an underground explosion while on a rescue mission during the Penygraig mining disaster of January 1884, an incident which was described in a broadsheet widely circulated at the time. The first of six verses of a poem (reproduced in Ken Llewellyn's book *Disaster at Tynewydd*, 1975) went like this:

> At Pennygraig [*sic*] Colliery a few days ago
> Many poor miners in death were laid low,
> Among the brave men whose spirits have flown,
> There was one gallant hero whose name is well-known;
> We mean Daniel Thomas, who the Queen's Medal wore,
> His life he had risked many times before,
> He always was ready when danger was near,
> In going down the coal mine he never show'd fear.

His chest tomb, surrounded by rusty railings and brambles, is near the road.

LLANTRISANT

On 13 January 1884, Wales's most celebrated eccentric **Dr William Price** (1800–93) conveyed the body of his illegitimate infant son, Iesu Grist ('Jesus Christ'), to Caerlan Field, Llantrisant, where he proceeded to cremate him. Alerted by a hostile crowd the local police arrested him but at his subsequent appearance at the Cardiff Assizes he was acquitted of the charge of burning his son, thereby establishing cremation as a legal act. After his own death nine years later, Price was cremated in a sheet-iron casket of his own design on the top of Caerlan Field in the presence of 20,000 onlookers, with his family selling souvenirs. On the wall of what was Zoar chapel down in the town, but is now a block of luxury flats, is a small brass tablet erected by the Cremation Society and the Federation of British Cremation Authorities, commemorating Price's place in history, and unveiled by his daughter Penelopen in 1947. Up the hill, in the Bull Ring, stands a statue of William Price, designed by Peter Nicholas.

LLANWONNO

By the church door in St Gwynno's churchyard is the grave of one of the greatest runners ever, if the stories are true. The achievement for which **Griffith Morgan** (1700–37), **Guto Nyth-brân**, is best remembered took place in September 1737 when he ran a twelve-mile race against an opponent known as 'The Prince' from Newport to Bedwas in the astonishing time of fifty-three minutes. Arriving at the winning post his girlfriend slapped him so hard on his back that he dropped dead on the spot. Guto's name is still honoured in the annual Nos Galan races held in Mountain Ash. Llanwonno and its pub, the Brynffynnon Arms, were among the favourite places of **Gwyn Thomas** (1913–81), the writer and broadcaster, and after his death his ashes were scattered on the grassy hillside some fifty yards from Guto Nyth-brân's grave.

MOUNTAIN ASH

Stephen Owen Davies (1886–1972), excluded from the Congregationalist Brecon Memorial College as a young man because his religious beliefs were too radical, was the very independent-minded MP for Merthyr Tydfil from 1934 until his death. As a committed socialist he was often in conflict with the domestic and foreign policies of successive Labour governments of his day and, because of the government's handling of the Aberfan disaster, he refused to be present when Harold Wilson was given the freedom of Merthyr Tydfil, despite being the local MP. A keen supporter of Welsh self-government, he was pleased to act as one of Gwynfor Evans's sponsors when he entered the Commons in 1966, not that this endeared him to his Labour colleagues. Finally deselected by the party before the 1970 general election, S. O. Davies romped to victory as an Independent Socialist. He is buried at the east end of section B (plot 669) of Maes-yr-arian cemetery, the second section to the left of the main entrance.

The Victorian statesman **Henry Austin Bruce, 1st Baron Aberdare** (1815–95) is buried at Aberffrwd cemetery, known as the 'old' cemetery. Liberal MP for Merthyr Tydfil from 1852 to 1868 and for Renfrewshire from 1868 to 1873 he was a controversial Home Secretary in Gladstone's first administration, introducing reforms to the licensing laws which pleased nobody. Elevated to the House of Lords in 1873, much of his subsequent career was devoted to educational matters, notably serving as chairman of an influential committee to inquire into intermediate and higher education in Wales. He became the first president of the University College of

South Wales and Monmouthshire in 1883, and in 1895 the first chancellor of the federal University of Wales. The family plot, which also contains the graves of the 2nd and 3rd Barons, is about thirty yards to the left at the point where the main path from the cemetery gate levels out before descending. About 100 yards along the path running left from the gate is a prominent Celtic cross (one of the tallest monuments in the cemetery) marking the grave of **John Nixon** (1815–99), a major coal proprietor in the south Wales valleys, owning Navigation, Mountain Ash, Merthyr Vale and Deep Dyffryn collieries. When he died he left over one million pounds, but not

John Nixon, Mountain Ash

a penny to charity. Towards the top end of the cemetery are many reminders of the fragility of human life in the valleys of south Wales in the late nineteenth century. One grave records the deaths of five Evans children between 1866 and 1878, one aged five, another aged three, and three more only a few months old.

PENDERYN

Like many of the great engineers of the nineteenth century **William Menelaus** (1818–82) was a Scotsman. He was general manager of the Dowlais ironworks for over thirty years during a time of unprecedented technical innovation. He was the first president of the South Wales Institute of Engineers; in 1875, in recognition of his national standing, he became president of the Iron and Steel Institute; and in 1881 he was awarded the Bessemer Gold Medal for his services to the iron and steel industry. In his spare time he built up an impressive collection of paintings which (to the disgust of the people of Merthyr) he bequeathed to Cardiff. This bequest is regarded as the foundation of the now world-famous art collection in the National Museum of Wales, where Menelaus's marble bust has an honoured place. Menelaus's sadly neglected chest-tomb is to the right of the main path in St Cynog's churchyard, south-east of the church. However, inside the church is a fine stained-glass window to his memory.

PONTYPRIDD

Evan James (1809–78), owner of a woollen factory in Pontypridd and a keen poet, wrote the words of what became the Welsh National Anthem, his son composing the tune. It is said that the first airing of the song was by Evan James in the Castell Ivor public house in Hopkinstown early in 1856. It is certain that the first public performance was given by Elizabeth John, a sixteen-year-old girl from Pontypridd, in Tabor Presbyterian chapel, Maesteg, later in the same year. For some years the song continued to be known by its original title 'Glan Rhondda' but by the 1880s it had become so popular at eisteddfodau and concerts that it became known throughout Wales as 'Hen Wlad fy Nhadau'. On his death, Evan was buried in the cemetery of Carmel chapel, Pontypridd, but in 1972, following the demolition of the chapel, the remains of Evan and his wife, and the original tombstone, were relocated to the foot of Sir William Goscombe John's memorial to Evan and his son in Ynysangharad Park.

John Thomas (1795–1871), radical journalist, teacher and, known as **Ieuan Ddu**, the finest choral conductor of his day, is buried in the centre of that section of St Mary's parish churchyard, Glyntaf, which lies to the right of the path from the main gate. He is generally hailed as the person who introduced Handel's Messiah to Wales in the 1840s. His grave is marked by a handsome Celtic cross, erected by his friends and pupils, and bears this warm tribute:

> Possessed of great and varied abilities and extensive information upon more than one science, his genius shone pre-eminently as a musical composer and critic of great taste and judgment. He was the first to lay the foundations of that prevailing taste for music, which attained its triumph in the Crystal Palace in the years 1872 and 1873.

Down the road from the parish church is Glyntaf cemetery and crematorium. The spectacularly tall memorial near the main entrance, by far the highest monument in the cemetery, marks the grave of **Walter Morgan** (1855–1901), one of the leading solicitors in south Wales (Morgan, Bruce and Nicholas of Pontypridd) and for some years vice-chairman of Glamorgan County Council. A prominent Liberal, he twice unsuccessfully stood for Parliament, at Denbigh Boroughs in 1895 and, more controversially, at South Glamorgan in 1900 when he opposed (according to the newspapers of the time) 'a gallant gentleman when he was fighting his country's battles' in the Boer War. The strain of it all led to Morgan's premature death at the Pump House Hotel, Llandrindod Wells. His residence, Forest House, across the valley from the cemetery, once the home of the Crawshays, is now part of the University of Glamorgan. **Noah Ablett** (1883–1935), the greatest Marxist thinker to emerge from the south Wales valleys, was cremated here and his ashes were scattered on the garden of remembrance. Co-author of *The Miners' Next Step* (1912) and a leading advocate of class war, he struck terror in the hearts of the mine owners for a few years but, increasingly overwhelmed by alcohol, this selfless zealot died, a spent force, at the early age of fifty-two. There is a memorial to him and his wife on the exterior, north-facing, wall of the columbarium. Glyntaf crematorium, established in 1924, was the only crematorium in Wales for nearly thirty years (Cardiff's opened in 1953), and in the North Chapel there is a stained-glass memorial window to Dr William Price, unveiled in October 1966 by his daughter **Penelopen**. After her death in 1977, aged 91, she was cremated here, her ashes scattered on plot 2, as had been those of her brother

Nicholas, also known as **Iesu Grist** ('Jesus Christ') **the Second**, fourteen years earlier. Perhaps surprisingly, no plaque exists to their memory.

TALYGARN

George Thomas Clark (1809–98) was a major figure in the industrial and cultural life of Victorian Wales. He ran the Dowlais ironworks after the death of Sir Josiah Guest and ensured the company's continuing prosperity for forty years, taking the major strategic decisions himself while leaving the day-to-day operations to gifted managers such as William Menelaus. Clark's overall importance to the iron industry was recognized by his election as the first president of the British Iron Trades Association in 1876. In his spare time he indulged in his lifelong interest in archaeology and medieval history, being instrumental in the formation of the Archaeological Association (later to become the Royal Archaeological Institute). In 1856 he acquired Talygarn House and proceeded to transform a modest country house into one of the great mansions of south Wales. George Clark built St Ann's church, across the road from the house, in memory of his wife, and he is buried in the north-east corner of the churchyard, under a prominent Celtic cross.

TONYREFAIL

Inspired by John Elias, preaching in Pontypridd in 1814, **William Evans** (1795–1891) became one of the great personalities of Non-conformity in nineteenth-century Wales, known to his contemporaries as 'cloch arian Cymru' (the silver bell of Wales) because of his fine singing voice. A prodigious preacher, he was in great demand everywhere; in 1825 alone he delivered over 400 sermons to crowded meetings during a tour of Wales, travelling 4,000 miles on horseback. He was most closely associated with Capel-y-ton in Tonyrefail, where he preached his last sermon at the ripe old age of ninety-two. After a huge funeral, attended by all the leading Methodist ministers in Wales, he was buried in a chest tomb right outside the chapel door. Clara Novello Davies (Ivor's mother) was his granddaughter and in Dillwyn Lewis's history of Tonyrefail there is a photograph of her laying a wreath on her grandfather's tomb.

Next to the car park of the Tonyrefail Working Men's Club is a playground where Ainon Baptist chapel and cemetery used to be until the early 1990s. However, some of the gravestones have been retained, including a good example of a 'murder stone', this one commemorating the tragic death of **Jane Lewis**, aged 23, daughter of Isaac and Selina Lewis, prominent members of the local Baptist cause. She was stabbed to death one day in December 1862 by an unknown attacker, while walking home from chapel. The stone proclaims that:

> tho her blood is hitherto unavenged, attention is directed to the day when light will have shone on the mysterious occurrence and guilt be accorded its just reward. God lives – revenge is His.

TREALAW

To the left of the office by the main entrance to the cemetery, in section B (plot number C 317), in his stepfather's grave, lie the ashes of **Thomas George Thomas**, **Viscount Tonypandy** (1909–97). Born and brought up in extremely humble circumstances, George Thomas, inspired by his beloved 'Mam', rose to great heights. However he never lost the common touch, which made him one of the most popular politicians of his time (though his autobiography upset some of his more sensitive colleagues). Labour MP for Cardiff Central, then for Cardiff West from 1945 to 1983, he served as Secretary of State for Wales from 1968 to 1970, masterminding Prince Charles's investiture in 1969. However, his controversial views, robustly expressed, on Welsh Nationalism and devolution ensured that he did not return to the Labour Cabinet in 1974, much to his disappointment. Nevertheless, two years later, he was appointed Speaker of the House of Commons, a position that well suited his theatrical talents, and over the next seven years his voice, uttering the words 'Order, order', became one of the best known on radio. His last public appearances were in support of Sir James Goldsmith's fierce campaign against the European Union during the 1997 general election. Further up the hill, about 100 yards to the north-west of the chapel, are the ashes of George Thomas's good friend **Thomas Farr** (1913–86), placed in the elegant grave he had erected for his mother and father (section V, plot 506). Tommy Farr, whom George recalled selling vinegar from a horse and cart in the streets of Tonypandy, rose to become among the greatest of all British-born heavyweight boxers, best remembered for his epic fight against Joe Louis at New York's Yankee Stadium on 30 August 1937, when he lost on points. Farr also had a good singing voice and during his heyday recorded some pleasant ballads including 'Remember Me', when he was accompanied by George Formby on his ukulele. The inscription on his grave reads:

> I claim that man
> Is master of himself
> When he can stand life's blows and scars
> And leave this world a better place behind him.

The celebrated Welsh actor, Sir Stanley Baker (1928–76), was also a good friend of George Thomas, who once wrote: 'I have always felt that as two boys from the Rhondda we belonged together despite the difference in our ages.' Dying of lung cancer only a month after receiving a knighthood, Baker was cremated at Putney Vale but his ashes were brought back to the Rhondda and scattered on the hillside above Ferndale.

Leftwards of Tommy Farr's grave, at the western end of the main cemetery (section X, plot 876) is the now unmarked grave of the radical agitator and author **Lewis Jones** (1897–1939), Communist member of the Glamorgan County Council, a leader of the National Unemployed Workers' Movement, which organized the hunger marches during the 1930s, and a passionate anti-Franco campaigner during the Spanish Civil War. In January 1939 he died of a heart attack, having addressed thirty street meetings in one day in support of the failing republican cause. He is now probably best remembered as the author of two powerful novels about working-class life and struggle in the Rhondda, *Cwmardy* (1937) and *We Live* (1939). His secular funeral in Tonypandy was a huge affair, his coffin being draped with a flag presented by the Russian miners to their British comrades in 1926. Leading the singing of 'The Red Flag' at the graveside was Arthur Horner (1894–1968), the Communist President of the South Wales Miners' Federation. It is not recorded whether Horner took the opportunity to stand for a moment at the rather more elaborate grave (section X, plot 780) of his old adversary **David Watts Morgan** (1867–1933), a few yards downhill from Jones's grave. Morgan, a mining engineer who had rescued eighteen miners during the Senghennydd pit disaster in 1913, was a fiercely anti-Communist Labour MP for Rhondda East from 1918 until his death, and had defeated Horner twice, in the general elections of 1929 and 1931. Horner himself died in London in 1968 and was cremated at Golders Green. In the north-west extension of the cemetery (section K1, plot 170) lies the celebrated writer **James Kitchener Davies** (1902–52), best known for one of the finest Welsh-language poems of the twentieth century, 'Sŵn y Gwynt sy'n Chwythu' (the sound of the wind that's blowing), written while he was dying of cancer and broadcast shortly before his death. He had already achieved fame, or notoriety, throughout the United Kingdom in 1934, because his play *Cwm Glo* had been denied the prize at the National Eisteddfod because its content was considered offensive to Nonconformist sensibilities. Needless to say, the play was soon performed to packed houses all over the country and the actress who played the loose-moraled Marged at the Swansea production could not see what the fuss was about: 'Had the play been written in English no storm would have been raised.' About 100 yards up the hill from the cemetery chapel and a little way to the right (section R, plot 726) is a striking grey marble memorial to **William Evans** (1864–1934), owner of the 'Thomas and

William Evans (Corona), Trealaw

Evans' Welsh Hills factory in Porth. Stimulated by the introduction of home deliveries, the business became the greatest soft drinks company in the country, and in the 1920s the 'Welsh Hills' brand was changed to 'Corona' and the famous crown logo, formed of pop bottles, adopted (*coron* is the Welsh for crown). Though Evans became a wealthy man he remained close to the local community throughout his life. He donated Browydd Park (where his bronze bust stands) to the people of Porth as a public park. The Welsh Hills factory, derelict for many years, is now a pop factory of a different sort altogether, where pop music is produced. A little way to the right of the cemetery chapel is a handsome memorial to Daniel Thomas, hero of the Tynewydd and Penygraig mining disasters, erected by public subscription at the spot where many of the men killed at Penygraig were buried.

TREFOREST

Owen Morgan (1836?–1921), widely known as **Morien**, was a true eccentric. A journalist with the *Western Mail* for thirty years, he specialized in dramatic stories, and he came into national prominence in 1877 when his graphic reports on the Tynewydd mine disaster kept the Welsh reading public on the edge of their seats for several days. A follower of William Price, and described as 'oftener in the clouds than on solid earth', he immersed himself in druidism and wrote colourful if unreliable works of local history. At his funeral the archdruid of Wales ('Dyfed') declared that 'neither time nor circumstance had succeeded in smoothing Morien into conformity with the things around; he was not one of the crowd'. He was interred in the cemetery at Saron chapel – the newspapers confirm that – but his grave is not recorded. One assumes he was buried with his wife, whose resting place is marked by a brown marble memorial.

TREORCHY
William Abraham (1842–1922), generally known by his bardic name **Mabon**, and Liberal, then Labour, MP for the Rhondda from 1885 to 1920, dominated the miners' movement in the south Wales valleys for over thirty years. In 1898 he became the first president of the South Wales Miners' Federation. However his conciliatory approach in the conduct of industrial relations put him increasingly at odds with the militant mood of a new generation of miners' leaders before the First World War, and in 1913 he resigned the presidency, a year after he had become a Privy Counsellor, a sure sign of the British establishment's favour. When he died, in Pentre, in May 1922, he departed this world a lot richer than he had entered it, leaving an estate of over £32,000, a substantial fortune at the time – much to the dismay of many of his former trade union colleagues. Mabon's grave, in section F of the cemetery, is on the right, some little way along the path that runs sharp left from the main entrance. Further up the hill lies the young radical, **Ben Bowen** (1878–1903) who, during a short life dogged by ill health, was a collier, a Baptist minister (expelled from Moriah chapel, Pentre, for heresy) and a highly promising poet. After his untimely death, Elfed wrote of him: 'No one was more a child of the newer age in Wales than he; no one showed more distinctly the genuine spirit of poetry.' His grave, in the middle of section D, is marked by a tall, slender obelisk of brown marble which cannot be missed. Right at the very top of the cemetery (plot K 753) is the grave of that great son of Gelli, **Roy Paul** (1920–2002), one of the finest wing-halves of his era, captain of Manchester City's cup-winning team of 1956 and capped thirty-three times for Wales. After his retirement he confessed that, as a Manchester City player, he had once accepted a £500 bribe to 'fix' a match (he had originally asked for £1,000): 'It was a risk but I needed the money.' No action was ever taken against him.

SWANSEA

CHERITON

In the churchyard of this Gower village lies **Ernest Jones** (1879–1958), the eminent psychoanalyst, who befriended Sigmund Freud, played a part in getting him out of Austria following the Nazi invasion in 1938 and who, in the 1950s, wrote Freud's definitive biography. A proud Welshman, Jones was an early member of Plaid Cymru. He once wrote, rather extravagantly: 'Coming myself from an oppressed race it was easy for me to identify myself with the Jewish outlook.' His first wife was the prodigiously talented composer Morfydd Llwyn Owen who died tragically young.

LOUGHOR

In the small cemetery behind Moriah chapel lies **Evan Roberts** (1878–1951) who, though never an ordained minister, was the central figure of the Welsh religious revival of 1904/5 which started in his home town of Loughor and spread like wildfire throughout the country. Loughor became for a short time a place of pilgrimage for visitors from Europe and America and the lives of thousands were touched by the phenomenon, many permanently. However, the revival ended as quickly as it had started. By the end of 1905 it was over; Evan Roberts, exhausted, retreated at the age of twenty-seven into a secluded existence that would last more or less for the rest of his life, and he died, impoverished, in Cardiff in 1951. His achievement, though short lived, is commemorated by a memorial in the front of Moriah chapel, unveiled two years after his death.

MORRISTON

Daniel James (1847–1920), a popular poet generally known by his bardic name **Gwyrosydd**, is buried in the cemetery of Mynydd-bach Independent chapel. One of the poems which appeared in his second collection of verse, published in 1892, was that eternal favourite 'Calon lân' (a pure heart), with the opening line 'Nid wy'n gofyn bywyd moethus' (I do not ask for a life of luxury). Though the words can be sung to the tune to 'What a friend we have in Jesus', they are usually sung to the rousing tune composed by John Hughes (1872–1914) of Landore, Swansea. A memorial plaque commemorating Gwyrosydd's contribution to the cultural life of Wales was erected outside the Treboeth Community Hall in 1936, and is much more accessible than his grave in the cemetery, now overwhelmed by Japanese knotweed and brambles.

Mynydd-bach Independent chapel cemetery, Morriston

Among those who have taken their last journey to Morriston crematorium was the Welsh rugby legend **Carwyn James** (1929–83), coach of the British Lions during their victorious tour of New Zealand in 1971, who died of a heart attack in an Amsterdam hotel, a disappointed man, in January 1983. His ashes were scattered on garden number 5 at the crematorium.

OYSTERMOUTH

In the western section of All Saints churchyard, marked by a chest tomb, is the grave of **Thomas Bowdler** (1754–1825) who was undoubtedly the Mary Whitehouse of his day. Born near Bath and living for most of his life in England, he settled near Swansea in 1810. In 1818, exploiting his surgical skills (he was a qualified doctor), he published an edition of Shakespeare with an intriguing title: *The Family Shakespeare in ten volumes; but those words and expressions are omitted which cannot with propriety be read aloud in a family*. Moreover, as he said in the introduction, there were also in his view many frivolous allusions to the scriptures which 'call imperiously for their erasement'. Although he played havoc with the text and attracted the scorn of literary critics, Bowdler's expurgated Shakespeare sold extremely well, going into four editions before his death. Gibbon's *History of the Decline and Fall of the Roman Empire* was similarly purified. The verb to 'bowdlerize' first appeared in print in 1836. Ironically, his tomb has two worthy quotations from the Bible extolling the sanctity of the truth. The story goes that on the anniversary of his birth or death, many years ago, Kingsley Amis and Wynford Vaughan-Thomas solemnly laid a wreath of fig leaves on the tomb.

119

When **Morfydd Llwyn Owen** (1891–1918) died, Professor David Evans, her former music teacher in Cardiff, lamented:

> I regard her early death as an incalculable loss to Welsh music – indeed I know of no young British composer who showed such promise.

She carried off all the best music prizes of her day including the Royal Academy of Music's blue riband for composition, the Charles Lucas Silver Medal. During her time in London, this gentle Presbyterian girl from Treforest was lionized by the London Welsh 'establishment' as well as by the London cosmopolitan set, mingling with D. H. Lawrence, Ezra Pound and Prince Yusupov, Rasputin's assassin. Her short and uneasy marriage to the celebrated psychoanalyst Ernest Jones ended with her sudden death from appendicitis. Her grave (section E, number 20) is marked by a Celtic cross, in an elevated position towards the top left corner of Oystermouth cemetery, from the mortuary chapel. Also in the cemetery (number M 138) is the grave of the Welsh sporting legend **William John Bancroft** (1871–1959). From 1890 to 1901 he made thirty-three consecutive rugby appearances for Wales at full-back, captaining the team twelve times and winning the Triple Crown once. He also became Glamorgan's first professional cricketer in 1896, more or less holding the struggling minor counties team together on his own before the First World War. Following his retirement in 1914 he continued to coach future Glamorgan stars, notably the great Gilbert Parkhouse.

PENNARD

Harri Webb (1920–94), poet, journalist and radical republican, is buried in the north-eastern section of the churchyard, near to the wall. Well known for his appearances on the BBC Wales television programmes *Poems and Pints*, some may also remember him as the designer of the logo later adopted by the Free Wales Army, the White Eagle of Eryri. Inside the church itself, on the north wall, is a plaque in memory of **Vernon Watkins**

(1906–67), a good friend of Dylan Thomas while he was alive and a vigorous defender of his reputation after his death. The plaque carries some words written by Watkins in Thomas's memory: 'Death cannot steal the light that love has kindled, nor the years change it.' Watkins was himself highly regarded as a poet and at the time of his death he was being seriously considered as a possible Poet Laureate. His ashes were scattered over the sea at Pennard, where he had lived for much of his life.

SKETTY

Inside St Paul's church, in the family crypt beneath the Vivian chapel, lies **Sir Henry Hussey Vivian** (1821–94), head of the Hafod copper-smelting works which made Swansea the metallurgical capital of the world during the second half of the nineteenth century, ruining the health of many of its citizens in the process. He resented the efforts of inspectors to improve conditions in the workplace:

> I need not say that there is and must be a great dislike upon the part of any manufacturer to have inspectors running over his works with power to go anywhere they please, and spy into everything they like. I want no one to come into our works unless I choose to allow him.

He was active in politics, first as Liberal MP for Truro (1852–57), for Glamorgan (1857–85) and for Swansea (1885–83). In 1887, tens of thousands of Welsh Liberals paraded past Sir Hussey's neo-Gothic house, Singleton Abbey (now the administration block of the University of Wales Swansea) to honour W. E. Gladstone who was staying there at the time. In 1889, Sir Hussey became the first chairman of Glamorgan County Council, and in 1893 he was elevated to the peerage as Baron Swansea. On the north side of the churchyard is the Dillwyn family plot, the resting place of **Lewis Llewelyn Dillwyn** (1814–92), another of Swansea's leading industrialists, and MP for the town from 1855 until his death. He was very much on the radical wing of the Liberal party, a pacifist, 'little Englander' and (though an Anglican himself) a leading figure in the campaign to disestablish the Church of England. Buried in the family plot are the ashes of his remarkable daughter **Elizabeth Amy Dillwyn** (1845–1935). A woman of independent spirit, she wrote popular novels in the 1880s in which she conveyed the frustrations of women trying to get on in a man's world and, as a regular book reviewer for the *Spectator*, could claim (with others) credit for recognizing the genius of Robert Louis Stevenson. One reason why she liked *Treasure Island* so much was 'that there is not a vestige of love-making in the whole book'. On her father's death she took over the running of his ailing spelter works in Llansamlet, turning it into a thriving business, so that in 1906 the *Western Mail* could describe her as 'one of the most remarkable women in Great Britain'. Though the business did not survive the post-war recession, her achievement as a woman in a man's world was widely acclaimed, and in 1982 the Amy Dillwyn Society erected a plaque on her grave 'to honour the memory of the First Woman Industrialist'. **Donald Coleman** (1926–91), Labour MP for Neath from 1964 until his death, is buried in the north-east section of the churchyard.

SWANSEA CITY CENTRE
In the cemetery of the now boarded-up Bethesda Baptist chapel in Prince of Wales Road, and marked by a handsome memorial near the chapel door, is the resting place of the formidable one-eyed preacher **Christmas Evans** (1766–1838), the dominant Baptist force in Anglesey for thirty-five years and acknowledged during his tours of Wales as the most powerful orator of his time. Gwilym Hiraethog described the phenomenon thus:

> Evans was aglow throughout, like the volcano Etna, or Vesuvius, casting out his lava like a seething river over his listeners, until all their emotions were aroused and became aflame in his overwhelming intensity. His power of imagination was unequalled, he would personify his subject matter before his hearers so as almost to force them to grasp it.

TORFAEN

LLANTARNAM
Just to the right of the entrance to St Michael's churchyard is the grave of **John William Fielding** (1857–1932), who ran away from home in 1877 and, using the name John Williams so that his family could not find him, joined the 24th Army Regiment at Monmouth. In the following year the regiment was posted to South Africa and, for his gallantry during the battle of Rorke's Drift in January 1879, an ordeal which turned his hair prematurely white, Fielding (portrayed by Peter Gill in the film *Zulu*) was one of eleven soldiers awarded the Victoria Cross, the largest number of such awards ever made after one battle. Following his discharge from the army in 1893

he continued to work as a civilian at Brecon barracks until his retirement in 1920. He remained a celebrity in and around Llantarnam until his death and his funeral was a grand affair, the cortège stretching for half a mile.

VALE OF GLAMORGAN

BARRY
(William James) Jimmy Wilde (1892–1969), known as 'the Mighty Atom' and 'the Tylorstown Terror' was one of Britain's greatest boxers, reigning as World flyweight champion from 1916 to 1923 and losing only four of 153 officially recorded fights, not to mention another 700 contests in the boxing booths. His simple grave ('ex-flyweight champion of the world') (N 991 in section N–O) is in the middle of Merthyr Dyfan municipal cemetery, and may be found by bearing right of the chapel near the cemetery entrance (where there is a useful site plan), and proceeding along the main tree-lined avenue to the left. He lies near to the seventh yew tree at the third turning to the right. At the fourth turning to the right is the grave (R 659) containing the ashes of **Gareth Jones** (1905–35), a Barry boy who, having studied at Aberystwyth, Cambridge and New York, became for a time the private secretary for foreign affairs to David Lloyd George in 1930. This gave him an exceptional opening in political circles, enabling him to become one of the most celebrated investigative journalists in the world, writing for the *Western Mail*, the *Manchester Guardian*, and other newspapers. In pursuit of a sensitive story about Japanese intentions in the Far East, he was murdered in Mongolia by bandits in sinister circumstances, never satisfactorily explained. His epitaph reads: 'He sought peace and pursued it.'

COWBRIDGE
Inside Holy Cross church, near to the altar on the south side, lies **Benjamin Heath Malkin** (1770–1842), the celebrated historian and traveller, best known for his book *The Scenery, Antiquities, and Biography of South Wales* (1804), drawing on two journeys undertaken in 1803, and which, in its coverage, historical detail and sheer interest, remains outstanding. He describes, for example, the pre-industrial Rhondda valleys where 'the contrast of the meadows, rich and verdant, with mountains the most wild and romantic, surrounding them on every side, is in the highest degree picturesque'. **Rice Merrick** (*c*.1520–86/7), another, earlier, historian,

author of *Morganiae Archaiographica: A Booke of Glamorganshire Antiquities*, is also said to be buried in the church, in the south aisle, though the memorial marking the spot has long since disappeared.

EWENNY

According to contemporary annalists, **Maurice de Londres**, lord of Ogwr, who lived during the first half of the twelfth century, 'excelled all other Barons of Wales in valiantness and liberality'. Victor over the gallant Welsh heroine Gwenllïan in 1136, it may have been in contrition for having executed her that he founded Ewenny priory, the finest example of Romanesque architecture in Wales, in 1141. The Norman-French inscription on his tomb in the south transept reads: 'God reward him for his services.'

FLEMINGSTON

Inside the church, on the north wall, a memorial carries a handsome tribute to that flawed genius **Edward Williams** (1747–1826), **Iolo Morganwg**, who is buried nearby. His mind expanded by painkilling drugs and acquainted with some of the leading scholars of his day, he combined fact and fantasy to construct a uniquely rich Welsh heritage full of bardic ritual, and in 1819 he linked his invention, the Gorsedd of Bards, to the eisteddfod tradition, thereby laying the foundations for the modern National Eisteddfod movement. In the words of his biographer, Professor G. J. Williams: 'Iolo gave to Wales a national institution.'

PENARTH

Joseph Parry, Penarth

A striking white marble memorial with musical motifs in the north-east section of St Augustine's churchyard marks the grave of **Joseph Parry** (1841–1903), Wales's most popular composer, the author of such well-loved hymn tunes as 'Aberystwyth', 'Sirioldeb' and 'Côr Caersalem', and of that evergreen melody 'Myfanwy'. His birthplace, Chapel Row, Merthyr Tydfil, is preserved as a museum in his memory, and Jack Jones's *Off to Philadelphia in the Morning* is a fictional account of aspects of his life. Also buried in the churchyard is the man who helped to lubricate the vocal chords of those who sang Parry's melodies. **Samuel Arthur Brain** (1850–1903) became the largest brewer and owner of public houses in Cardiff and his initials are still used to describe the company's premium beer, 'SA'. A major figure in the public life of Cardiff, he was mayor in 1899. His grave, surrounded by iron railings and marked by a slender stone cross, is located by the south-east corner of the church.

John Saunders Lewis (1893–1985), one of the great figures of twentieth-century Wales, is buried in the Roman Catholic section (section L, number 1), in the far right of Penarth cemetery when approached from the main gate. Acknowledged as a writer of European stature, his reputation in Wales is mainly based on two events. One was as one of the three Plaid Cymru activists (he was then the president of the party) who committed an act of arson at the Penyberth bombing range in 1936, leading to eventual imprisonment and dismissal from his academic post at the University College of Swansea. The other event was his historic radio lecture in 1962 on *Tynged yr Iaith* (The Fate of the Language) which led to the establishment of Cymdeithas yr Iaith Gymraeg (the Welsh Language Society) of which he became honorary president.

Lavernock Point, the place from where, in 1897, Marconi had transmitted wireless waves across water for the first time (to nearby Flat Holm island), was the spot where the ashes of the celebrated peace campaigner from Bedlinog, **Reverend Gwilym Davies** (1879–1955) were scattered. In 1922, he inaugurated the Message of Peace from the Children of Wales to the Children of the World which is proclaimed annually on 18 May, International Day of Goodwill. Gwilym Davies is also acknowledged as the first person to make a broadcast in Welsh, on St David's Day, 1923.

PENMARK

The parish church of St Mary the Virgin is said to be (though there is nothing in the church to confirm this) the resting place of **Colonel Philip Jones** (1618–74), Wales's leading Parliamentarian during the Civil War and virtual ruler of south Wales during the Protectorate. A close colleague of Oliver Cromwell, he served in the Upper or 'Other' House as Philip lord Jones and, as Controller of the Household, he was responsible for organizing Cromwell's funeral in 1658. Though some disgruntled royalists tried to have him brought to account for his activities during the years of the republic, Jones, never an extremist, managed to survive the Stuart restoration unscathed, prospering in his estates at Fonmon, and becoming High Sheriff of Glamorgan in 1671. A memorial plaque inside the church identifies other occupants of the family vault while outside, by the east perimeter wall of the churchyard, lie more recent descendants of Colonel Jones, including members of the Boothby dynasty who trace their baronetcy to 1644, and who have owned Fonmon castle since the 1930s. The **15th Baronet, Sir Hugo Robert Brooke Boothby** (1907–86), was made an honorary freeman of the Vale of Glamorgan and served for some years as Lieutenant of South Glamorgan.

PORTHKERRY

In the south-east corner of the churchyard is a small anonymous stone, no more than a foot high, marking the burial place of 'A Seafaring Man found Drowned 1866', a not uncommon headstone along the Welsh coast. Contrast this poignant stone with the formidable memorial, a few feet away, to **John Gaspard le Marchant, 3rd Baron Romilly** (1866–1905), landowner and captain in the Coldstream Guards.

ST ANDREWS MAJOR

Erith Gwyn Nicholls (1875–1939), though born in Gloucestershire, was, in the words of the *Western Mail*, 'a true son of Wales in everything but birth'. He is generally regarded as the greatest centre three-quarter of his day, a view from which he would not have dissented, being something of a prima donna. The fact remains that he scored 111 tries in 242 appearances for Cardiff, and gained twenty-four caps for Wales, leading them to two Triple Crowns as well as to the historic victory over the All Blacks in 1905. Following his retirement he prospered in the laundry business, while keeping in close touch with the game as a Welsh selector and as the author of a perceptive book, *The Modern Rugby Game and How to Play It*. He is buried across the road from the church, to the right of the path at the point where the path bears left. His name is spelt 'Gwynne' on his headstone.

ST HILARY

Just to the left of the church door is the grave of **John Charles Clay** (1898–1973), member of a Cardiff shipowning and coal-exporting family and every inch a true gentleman-sportsman. Owner of 'Charlie H', winner of the 1972 Welsh Grand National, he was one of the great Glamorgan County cricketers between 1921 and 1949, coming out of retirement in 1948 at the age of fifty to play an important part in Glamorgan's County Championship triumph. He played for England once, against South Africa in 1935, and over his whole career took 1,315 first-class wickets, mainly as an off-spinner, at an average of under twenty. In one game, against Worcestershire in 1937, he took seventeen wickets in the match. At various times Johnny Clay served Glamorgan as captain, secretary, treasurer and, from 1961 until his death, as its president. For a couple of years he was also an England selector.

ST NICHOLAS

A Cambridge blue and an occasional player for Cardiff in between injuries, **Cliff Jones** (1916–90) was widely considered the most dazzling star in British rugby during the 1930s. He won thirteen caps for Wales between 1934 and 1938, his greatest performance being in 1935 when he contributed brilliantly to Wales's 13–12 victory against the All Blacks. He captained the side in 1838. After the war he became a celebrated rugby administrator, acting as a national selector for over twenty years and pioneering the introduction of new coaching techniques and the concept of squad training into the Welsh game. It was fitting that he should serve as president of the Welsh Rugby Union during its centenary year, 1980–1. His grave, marked by a simple slate headstone, is in the south-west section of the churchyard. In the north-east section, under an altogether more elaborate chest-tomb, lie members of the 'Devonshire' Cory family (as opposed to the 'Cornwall' Corys who lie in Cathays cemetery). **John Cory** (1828–1910) was a wealthy shipowner, coalowner and philanthropist who built the present Dyffryn House and whose bronze statue, made by Sir William Goscombe John, was erected outside Cardiff City Hall in 1905.

WREXHAM

GLYN CEIRIOG

In the churchyard, to the left of the path from the main gate, lies **Stephen James Lake Taylor** (1910–88), politician and educationalist who, as a young doctor, was enthusiastically involved in the planning that led to the establishment of the National Health Service in 1948, and who published the influential book *Good General Practice.* He became Labour MP for Barnet in 1945 and served as parliamentary private secretary to Herbert Morrison, only to lose his seat to the young Reginald Maudling in 1950. In 1958, as one of the first batch of life peers, he entered the House of Lords as Lord Taylor of Harlow (he was an influential member of the Harlow New Town Development Corporation), and in 1964 he served briefly as a junior minister in Harold Wilson's first government, before becoming the first president and vice-chancellor of the Memorial University of Newfoundland in 1965. Like many others he became disillusioned with the post-Callaghan Labour party, becoming a cross-bencher in 1981, finding it 'impossible to adhere mentally to the decisions of democracy when they are manifestly wrong'.

MARCHWIEL

Probably the most prominent memorial in St Marcella's churchyard is the handsome Celtic cross marking the grave of **Sir Alfred David McAlpine** (1881–1944) who, during the 1920s and 1930s, developed that branch of the family firm which became synonymous with the building trade, both domestic and commercial, in north Wales and the north-west of England. He was particularly involved in projects such as upgrading the Manchester Ship Canal, the development of Ellesmere Port and the construction of the Mersey Tunnel. Knighted in 1932, Sir Alfred played an influential role in the political and cultural life of north Wales for thirty years and enjoyed some success as a racehorse owner. St Marcella's church, or its churchyard, is also the resting place of several generations of the **Yorkes**, a decent and considerate family who owned the Erddig estate from 1733 until 1973, when it passed into the hands of the National Trust.

RUABON

In Ruabon church there are several striking memorials to the seventeenth- and eighteenth-century members of the influential Williams Wynn family, the uncrowned 'kings' of north Wales. The most formidable member of the dynasty was undoubtedly the third baronet, **Sir Watkin Williams Wynn** (1693–1749), a reactionary Tory who ran his fiefdom with a rod of iron from his stately home at Wynnstay. MP for Denbighshire, he was one of the leading Jacobites in the House of Commons though during the Jacobite Rebellion of 1745 he kept his head down, preferring to wait on events, much to the disgust of Bonnie Prince Charlie. It is said that, after his death in a hunting accident, his wife hurriedly destroyed any incriminating correspondence regarding his Jacobite con-nections. He is commemorated by a fine memorial by the sculptor

A Wynn family memorial, Ruabon

J. M. Rysbrack near to his resting place. Elsewhere in the church are the remains of local businessman and landowner **George Hammond Whalley** (1813–78), buried in the family vault not far from a commemorative plaque. Whalley, MP for Peterborough from 1852 until his death, was a fanatical anti-Catholic who believed that the Jesuits were the root of all evil, a point of view that led him to become one of the leading champions of the Tichborne Claimant, a rogue who claimed to be the long-lost heir to the Tichborne baronetcy and estates. Whalley alleged in campaigns up and down the land that the Roman Catholic establishment (the Tichbornes were a leading Catholic family) were out to deny the claimant his rightful inheritance. After two long and celebrated court cases which gripped the public imagination, Arthur Orton, son of a Wapping butcher, was imprisoned for ten years as an impostor in 1874, while Whalley had already been fined £250 for contempt of court and would have gone to jail himself if his sister had not paid the fine.

WREXHAM

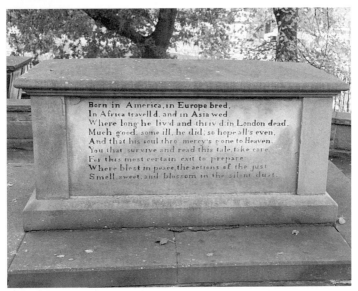

Elihu Yale, Wrexham

Born in Connecticut of Welsh ancestry **Elihu Yale** (1649–1721) came to Wales as an infant. After a London education he joined the East India Company in Madras in 1670, rising to become governor of the company from 1688 to 1699, during which time he made a fortune. He retired to Plas Grono, Wrexham, his ancestral home (demolished in 1876) where he was a generous supporter of local causes. He is immortalized however through his benefaction of books, pictures and money to the college at New Haven, which in 1745 took the name of Yale University. Yale is buried in St Giles's churchyard by the west door and the epitaph on his tomb, restored by Yale University in 1874, reads:

> Born in America, in Europe bred,
> In Africa travell'd and in Asia wed,
> Where long he liv'd and thriv'd; in London dead.
> Much good, som ill he did, so hope all's even
> And that his soul, thro mercy's gone to heaven.
> You that survive and read this tale, take care,
> For this most certain exit to prepare,
> Where, blest in peace the actions of the just
> Smell sweet, and blossom in the silent dust.

The great Welsh Puritan **Morgan Llwyd** (1619–59), author of the classic work of mysticism *Llyfr y Tri Aderyn* (The Book of the Three Birds), was buried in Rhos-ddu Dissenting burial ground, where a memorial was unveiled by Mrs David Lloyd George in 1912. In 1960, the cemetery was adopted by the borough council and converted into the Morgan Llwyd Memorial Park. Though he regarded Charles I as a tyrant who got his just deserts, and for a while was associated with the ultra-radical fifth monarchist movement, Llwyd ultimately took the side of the moderates against the extremists during the Protectorate, believing that no one had a monopoly on the truth. His egalitarian instincts extended to his view of society. As an 'approver' in Wales during the Commonwealth period, responsible for selecting effective preachers to replace discredited royalist clerics, he encountered much criticism from the gentry for being prepared to select seemingly ill-educated and ill-bred preachers who might threaten the stability of the social structure. He even went so far as to observe: 'No poor man shall have too little nor the rich too much.' Perhaps it is not surprising that, according to one account, a royalist soldier, clearly affronted by Llwyd's view of the world, visited his last resting place and thrust his sword into the grave up to the hilt.

INDEX